Praise for From My Hea

x

In choosing to title the book *From My Heart*, a reader might first think that this is a soppy attempt to do a 'motherhood and apple pie' job on education. However, by inviting us to embark on a virtual relationship with him, Neil takes the reader on an evidence-based journey getting to the heart of what education should be about – not grades and results, but what we as a society want a well-educated 18 or 19 year old to look like. Hawkes draws the reader into a journey, not in an airy-fairy way but gets to the nitty-gritty of how to model the values and behaviours we seek to develop in the next generation – a generation that is open and hasn't, as yet, been tainted by experience because, as Neil reminds us, it's never too late to have a happy childhood! I first heard Neil address the European School Heads Association Conference in Cyprus and was so impressed I invited him to Ireland. I was certain Irish school leaders were longing to hear someone who could articulate something that I know each individual felt in their own hearts about vision and values for society. I wasn't wrong and the feel-good factor that permeated conference following Neil's address to delegates lasted long after they returned to their schools. Neil's invitations to pause, his use of reflection points at the end of each chapter, his use of a positive values vocabulary, his descriptions of the impact of the adopted approaches on students and practitioners, his hints and suggestions about how to embed a values-based culture make this book a must-read for all who reflect on education, especially school leaders, teachers and those involved in the educational enterprise. I wholeheartedly recommend it – especially to those suffering from TBD (Too Busy Disorder).

Clive Byrne, Director of the National Association of Principals and Deputy Principals and Executive Board Member of the European School Heads Association

This book provides a sensitive and subtle invitation for readers to engage and reflect on their work in the world of education within which they work and live. This is a book which cannot and should not be ignored. Through Neil's detailed analysis, arising from extensive work in schools throughout the world, his message is clearly set out in a powerful vision that reminds us all of the human nature of the school experience and presents a call for how we can reignite and renew our sense of what schools can and should be – for all the children, the staff, the parents and the community served. The reader is gently reminded that in any institution, school or company, there should never be a hierarchy of relationships, only a hierarchy of roles.

Within such a powerful culture, and where it is clear that it is human relationships which matter most, then the real benefits arising from a 'talk together, plan together, work together' and a values-based philosophy and practice suddenly *all* becomes very clear…

Chris Harrison, Former President of the National Association of Head Teachers (2011–2012)

Neil Hawkes has been the fearless pioneer of values-based education – both as an outstanding head of school and then as a public educator. This book encapsulates the extraordinary power of his message.

Lord Richard Layard

Neil Hawkes has influenced not just the schools he has run, but countless others in using a values-based approach to change for the better the way children and their families lead their lives. Here he writes in a way that any school leader, in any country or setting, will find inspiring and practically useful in doing the same thing.

Professor Sir Tim Brighouse

At Wellington College, we believe that education is only of enduring meaning if it is underpinned by profound values, the five which our community itself has chosen being courage, integrity, respect, kindness and responsibility. I agree with Neil that values-based education should be the driving principle for all schools and colleges in the twenty-first century.

Dr Anthony Seldon, Master, Wellington College

Neil Hawkes manages to convey the vitality of values-based education, a set of principles that can guide the learning journeys for those who learn and those who teach. The best teachers recognise that they are learners too and this fundamental belief in individual growth shines through the book.

Mick Waters, Professor of Education, Wolverhampton University

This is an ideal teaching reference and guide for practical values-based education written by one of the world's foremost and most reputable values-based educators. Few people anywhere have the theory and practice of values-based education as synchronised or its effects as proven as Dr Neil Hawkes.

Terence Lovat, Emeritus Professor, University of Newcastle, Australia and Senior Research Fellow, University of Oxford

Neil Hawkes's vision is the change agent for values-based education we all need. This book provides the insight for us to move from 'talking the talk' to 'walking the walk' and is a must-read for parents and educators.

Sue Cahill, Student Well-Being Leader, St Charles Borromeo Primary School, Melbourne, Australia

Rooted in his own experiences as a successful teacher and head teacher, the author has a deep commitment to core human values being placed at the heart of good and great schools. In this book, he draws upon his extensive international work to offer a carefully argued and convincing rationale as to why school leaders – and indeed business and wider society – might embrace the practical ideas he puts forward.

Roy Blatchford, Director, National Education Trust

I have always looked at the art of leadership as being one of self-awareness and an awareness of others. As Sun Tsu fabulously puts it, 'Leadership is a matter of intelligence, trustworthiness, humaneness, courage, and discipline. Reliance on intelligence alone results in rebelliousness. Exercise of humaneness alone results in weakness. Fixation on trust results in folly. Dependence on the strength of courage results in violence. Excessive discipline and sternness in command result in cruelty. When one has all five virtues together, each appropriate to its function, then one can be a leader.' Neil has been able to bring the skill of understanding all components to children, educators and parents, and without doubt has made a difference to our world through his delivery of values-based education, and I thank him for that.

Floyd Woodrow MBE DCM

Neil Hawkes writes lucidly, and with an infectious encouragement, about what he has been doing as a teacher, leader and advocate for at least the last twenty years. The quality of education provided for children, students and their families has been the cornerstone of his work, based as it has always been on their growing commitment to the values his schools have selected and celebrated. To hear and read, as I have often done, about what the children are learning and discussing about a whole range of values, and how this has helped their development and, importantly, how often this has changed their lives, is all in this book. It is a 'life enhancer'.

Richard Howard, Chair, National Education Trust

Guided and inspired by Neil, values-based education now pervades Ratton School. Exploring the meaning of our values and judging ourselves against them has brought clarity of purpose and a common understanding to our work. As a result, staff motivation and student behaviour have improved. Our values-based education has also proved popular with parents, who cite our strong values as a reason why they want their children to be a part of our school.

David Linsell, Head Teacher, Ratton School, Eastbourne

Being successful in school requires good teachers, but mostly you need a humane approach among adults and students. Each student must feel that they can succeed. To create this, you need a values-based curriculum that involves all aspects of work, which is the essence of Dr Hawkes's philosophy and practice. His approach does not require expensive materials or long education. However, it is an easy way to work with the positive values with which we want to permeate learning. Values-based education is an ideal approach that fits well in schools in Sweden.

Anna Sundström, Head of Education, Skövde, Sweden

I have had the pleasure of working with Dr Neil Hawkes in New Zealand, where he has addressed numerous principals' organisations, and in the UK where I visited schools that have embedded his values-based philosophy. With the emphasis on values in the New Zealand curriculum, this book provides teachers and others involved in the education of our young people with an insight into both the philosophy behind values-based education and the key steps to take to enable it within their educational environment. Neil's approach is warm, enlightening and encouraging.

Paul Daley, Principal, Sancta Maria College, Auckland, New Zealand

Values-based education is at the heart of everything we do here at Chantry Primary Academy. Guided by Neil's inspirational work, our staff team are driven by our values in the way they teach, and how they support our children and their families, resulting in comments like this from one of our pupils: 'Values have helped me with schoolwork and friendship. The values link and help Chantry to never let me down, they always believe in you.' Our strong values have enhanced our school's excellent reputation in the community, helped us to become an even better school and are a core element of our school's 'personality'. We will continue to learn and to grow in our values journey with Neil's work to support us.

Corisande Bateman, Head Teacher, Chantry Primary Academy, Luton

As an ex-head teacher of a values-based school and now the values education coordinator for Bedfordshire, I have twelve years first-hand experience of the positive and inspirational impact of Neil's work in all phases of education. This book will support and re-energise those schools already involved in values education, whilst inspiring and encouraging those setting out on their values journeys.

Diana Thomas, Values Education Coordinator, Bedfordshire

Great schools are hatcheries for good souls. To do this, the centre point of schools needs to be value-based education. Neil's book will not only help you live these values, it will help you to weave and embed them into the tapestry of the culture of your school.

Andrew Fuller, Clinical Psychologist and Family Therapist, Melbourne, Australia

Values-based education has enriched my personal life and the lives of my students, as well as my professional life as a teacher. It influences the way an individual tackles life's experiences and how they deal with the various obstacles of life. It offers a new perspective, and requires the teacher to have integrity and to be true to his values. This teaching method makes the individual more aware of his own feelings and those of others. Values-based education awakens us to the inner values of life. By working with these values, teachers become better at their profession and the students blossom in a new and wondrous way. Mutual respect, cooperation and unity are qualities that represent those who sincerely apply values-based education in their personal and professional life. Applying values-based education, as a teacher and as a human being, is character building and constructive for society.

Valgerður Knútsdóttir, Head Teacher, Leikskolinn Alfaheidi, Iceland

No matter what stage of the life-long journey of exploring or implementing values-based learning you are on, and irrespective of how much personal and professional experience you, your school or organisation has in this field, you need to touch base with Neil's expertise. In Brunei, we have benefitted from working within a unique combination of cultures and environments. Our success over the years is built on our ability to transform lives through values in action. This approach powerfully reaches out to people of all cultures and faiths. It moves the spirit, touches the soul and is a guiding light for all who want to make a difference to their own and other's lives. From Brunei, 'The Abode of Peace', our message is a simple one – get inspired through taking the time to read and take action!

Kathy Wood MBE MEd, Head Teacher, Hornbill School, Brunei

Dr Neil Hawkes demonstrates again and again that he has important insights into character education. I highly recommend this book.

Professor William Jeynes, Senior Fellow, Witherspoon Institute, Princeton and

Professor, Department of Education, California State University

As a head teacher who has led two values-based schools, I am totally indebted to the work of Dr Neil Hawkes in the development of values-based education as it has had such a profound effect on me both professionally and personally. Values-based education has provided me with a strong fundamental base from where I have been able to build my leadership skills, especially with regard to developing people and forging positive relationships. The shared common language of values-based education gives everyone in a values-based community a clear understanding of expectations and the opportunity to explore the evolving nature of our individual moral compasses based on our experiences.

Dr Hawkes has been pivotal in this journey as his philosophy is to gently challenge our thoughts, words and actions. As our school embeds a values-based education approach to living and learning together, Dr Hawkes has had a presence, probing deeply into our thought patterns so that we reflect, analyse and take responsibility in making positive changes to ourselves.

I am truly delighted that Dr Hawkes is now sharing this journey through this wonderful book, *From My Heart*, transforming lives through values. As Megan, one of my former pupils once said to me, 'If anyone wants to have a happy life they should simply use values-based education. It will help them to live a long and happy life.' I can't think of a better way to endorse this book.

Julie Rees, Head Teacher, Ledbury Primary School, Herefordshire

I have been a head teacher for eleven years and led two schools using values-based education. This 'way of being' in school permeates every aspect of school life and thus school improvement. I could not imagine, especially in the current educational climate, leading a school without a rigorous bedrock of values-led relationships leading to values-led learning. As a consequence of this, there is a depth of metacognitive learning, learning of real beauty and worth, woven into the fabric of places called schools, giving a strong moral direction ensuring the flourishing of all.

Julie Carr, Head Teacher, Lyneham Primary School, Wiltshire

Neil's experience as a leading educator shines through this book which is both intensely practical and profound. Leaders of schools, corporate organisations and communities will gain insight into how to be truly self-managing by identifying shared values, and then using these to evaluate success. What Neil demonstrates in this book is how to go about creating and inhabiting a shared language for values education which is local, accessible and powerful.

Dr Ruth Deakin Crick, Reader in Systems Learning and Leadership, University of Bristol

Neil Hawkes is an inspirational colleague. As soon as I met Neil, I realised that he had a special message, and indeed a special gift, to share with anyone who passionately cares about the education of children. His message and mantra advocating a values-based educational approach, is both timely and powerful. Anyone who has used values-based education within their school will tell you that mutual respect and trust is built through paying attention to the way people discuss, define and model their shared values. These explicit debates and agreements lead, if successfully and determinedly adhered to and modelled, a school community that is built on trust and interdependency. This is the strong 'glue' that makes schools successful. However, make no mistake, Neil does not advocate a 'fluffy', poorly defined culture where relationships take centre stage for their own sake. This is the building block whereby top quality educational experiences for children are focused upon and ensured, and, most importantly, raising achievement and life chances for children is at the top of the agenda. I unreservedly recommend that all school leaders, from primary and secondary schools, read this book and act on its wisdom. Also, invite Neil, who is an inspirational speaker, to visit your setting for a thought provoking and practice changing event!

Sue Woodrow, Head Teacher, Aylestone Secondary School, Hereford

In 2010 I had the privilege to hear Neil speak about the purpose of values-based education at an international convention for European school principals in Cyprus.

I was deeply touched by Neil's inspiring lecture. He provided the answer and the confirmation that we should not focus on learning and cognitive results alone, at a time when the tendency in the Netherlands was to overemphasise cognitive achievements only.

As a result of this conference we decided to organise an Inspiration Day in October 2012 for more than 1,000 teachers in Helmond, for which we invited Neil and his wife Jane to speak about values-based education. This Inspiration Day marked the start of 'a quiet revolution' within the Helmond educational community. Individual teachers started thinking about ways to pay more attention in their classrooms to values-based education and the holitisic development of children. Also, at a city level, we launched a task group to offer a more structural approach towards values-based education for the Helmond school community.

I therefore wholeheartedly recommend this inspirational book to anyone who, like us in the Netherlands, believe that education should be more than just about learning outcomes. For each and every child, a well-balanced education that includes the development of values will contribute to better learning achievements, which will ultimately result in a more peaceful and values conscious society.

Dr Erik Wissink, Psychologist/Manager,
OCGH Advies (Education Consultancy), Helmond

Values-based education, as described in Neil's inspirational and practical book, has had a huge impact on the children at Tower Hill Primary School. Initially the reasons for its implementation were to address the children's social and emotional needs through an approach that we felt would have a greater impact than SEAL or PHSCE. As soon as the new values became embedded, we began to notice rapid changes in the behaviour of the children and their relationships towards each other. This in turn, has had a phenomenal impact upon attainment and progress. An open and supportive culture now pervades all aspects of learning, where real and appropriate self-assessment, peer and teacher assessment are used to further enhance the learning. Suggestions for the improvement of work and behaviour are no longer seen as criticism, but are welcomed by each child and acted upon accordingly. The direct result of implementing values-based education is a happy school, where learners thrive on a mutually supportive atmosphere and learning has been rapidly accelerated as a result.

Tracey Smith, Head Teacher,
Tower Hill Community Primary School, Witney, Oxfordshire

This book, like all of Neil's work, comes from the heart, and what he advocates is also supported by powerful evidence and a strong understanding of practice in schools. This unique combination enables practitioners to be confident that it will help them to improve their practice and the lives of the children they work with, and their own lives as well. Neil's generosity of spirit shines through all his work and this is no exception. It has the potential to radically change how and what we do in our schools.

Dr Hilary Emery, Chief Executive, National Children's Bureau

Dr Neil Hawkes's book comes at an opportune moment in history. It is a wake-up call to live our lives more meaningfully and, in doing so, to inspire others. Neil writes with depth, compassion and wisdom drawn from his many years of experience and experiential knowledge of values education. It is a must read for all educators who believe in taking their students to greater heights. Research has conclusively proven that a values-based school brings out the best in students and teachers; implementing Neil's valuable, tested strategies will lead to excellence in all spheres.

Ruby Pardiwaller, Director, National Children's Council, The Seychelles

FROM MY HEART
TRANSFORMING LIVES THROUGH VALUES

Dr NEIL HAWKES

 Independent Thinking Press

First published by

Independent Thinking Press
Crown Buildings, Bancyfelin, Carmarthen, Wales, SA33 5ND, UK
www.independentthinkingpress.com

Independent Thinking Press is an imprint of Crown House Publishing Ltd.

First published 2013.

Cover image © Paddy Boyle.

British Library Cataloguing-in-Publication Data
A catalogue entry for this book is available
from the British Library.

Print ISBN 978-178135106-2
Mobi ISBN 978-178135116-1
ePub ISBN 978-178135117-8

Printed and bound in the UK by
TJ International, Padstow, Cornwall

Acknowledgements

Writing this book has been sheer joy, because it has seemed to write itself, with me watching with delight as each chapter unfolded. I think this apparent magic is mainly because the book brings to life the personal and working experiences I have enjoyed in the company of so many wonderful people in many countries. They have willingly and generously shared their insights and the good practices that they are developing as values-based people and educators. My role, in crafting this book, has been to capture this brilliance so that you and others can see the tremendously powerful effect that values-based education has on people, families, communities and nations.

I would like to acknowledge my debt of gratitude to the countless number of academics, head teachers, principals, teachers and support staff with whom I have worked in my various roles in education over the last forty years. These extraordinary people have shaped my philosophy and have made it possible for me to write this book. They include academic giants in moral education, such as Professors Richard Pring (Oxford), Bart McGettrick (Hope), Terry Lovat (Newcastle Australia), and Mark Halstead (Huddersfield), who have had a profound influence on my thinking about values education.

It would be inappropriate to single out any one teacher to mention because, in so doing, I would omit the thousands who have all played their part in influencing my thinking and practice. However, to all educators, my heartfelt thanks for your inspiration and encouragement which has allowed me to assume a role as the advocate for values-based education. Nevertheless, I would like to thank those individuals who have provided quotes for this book: Richard Barrett, Jeff Conquest, Simon Cowley, Cyril Dalais, Tracey Dennis, Michael Downey, Pete Dunmall, Sam Gardner, Katie Greenwood, Linda Heppenstall, Allison Hickson, David Jones, Sue Jones, Bridget Knight, David Linsell, Bart McGettrick, Sandra Mitchell, Cath Woodall, Simon Poote, Julie Rees, Rebecca Rees, Anthony Seldon, Eugene Symonds, Kathy Wood, Floyd Woodrow and Sue Woodrow.

At a personal level, I want to thank my wonderful family for their love, particularly my wife, Jane, who is a constant source of enthusiasm and loving support for my life's work.

Author's Letter

Dear Reader,

I have just finished writing the final chapter of this book and I am sitting in the lounge at our home overlooking Rutland Water. The ospreys have recently returned from overwintering in Africa, and I have a sense of awe and wonder as I watch a pair circling in the blue sky. The sun is shining on the water, creating diamond-like sparkles; the countryside seems full of expectant energy as spring finally arrives.

My mood and the scene I am witnessing give me a sense of the incredible privilege it is to be alive. I recall my brother, Maurice's, words, 'Remember, Neil, this is not a rehearsal; embrace life now.' My understanding is that people, just like you and me, have a huge potential to embrace life and to live in harmony with other people and our environment. However, we are all capable of sabotaging our potential happiness and well-being and the sustainability of our beautiful planet, and frequently do so. Is there an answer to this paradox?

Over the last thirty years, my life's mission has been to support others and myself to kindle a spark of goodness, which I believe resides in each of us. And, by so doing, embrace and release into the world the creative, dynamic energy of our innate human qualities, which include love, peace and compassion. I have also been acutely aware that such a desire to nourish virtuousness can appear idealistic and naive, failing to recognise the reality of our human condition.

Not to be deterred, I have engaged on a quest to find a practical philosophy that would make a contribution to the evolution of human consciousness. This mission has brought me into contact with many truly remarkable human beings who have supported me. The content of this book is witness to their wisdom, and I make no claims that my work is mine alone.

I believe that this book represents a modest contribution to helping each of us explore our human potential. In it, I invite you to discover the core philosophy and practices of what I have termed *valuing* and its practical application, *values-based education* (VbE).

The evidence that I will share with you, from many countries, is that values-based education is a powerful way to foster a values-based person, family, school, business, community, country and world.

I hope that you enjoy the experience of engaging with the ideas you will encounter on your journey through this book. They have changed my life; they may also change yours.

Warmest good wishes,

Neil

Contents

Chapter 1

You and me

Hello! Thank you for choosing to read my book, which is written 'from my heart'. It is unlikely that you know me, so here is a photo …

You   Me

Before reading my book, I would like to invite you to find a picture of you to put in the space next to mine or, if you prefer, make a sketch of yourself. You see, this book is about more than just reading a text: it is about you and me, and the relationship we can develop through the exploration of values which this book provides. I believe that good relationships are paramount – they help us to make sense of our complex world, and most of us desire them. They are the fundamental core principle of a values-based family, business and school.

Now, please may I request that you spend a minute or so just being still and quiet, thinking about what you sense about us both. You probably know very little about me, but you will know a great deal about you.

Pause ...

Thank you. I will explain later why it is so important for us to take moments of quiet reflection. I sense that you are someone who has chosen to read this book because you are conscious of your own personal journey through life; you are open to deepening your understanding about how you can help yourself and others to live life with a greater sense of inner peace and harmony.

I am sorry that I can't be with you personally; nevertheless, I have put the energy of loving good wishes, which I put into my talks about values, into this book. I often begin my talks by spending a little time in silence, just being still and gently making eye contact with individuals in the audience – hopefully each one. I know that some folk may think a variation of, 'Who the hell is this weirdo?' Others giggle or glance furtively at the person sitting next to them for reassurance, whilst others adopt a wry, expectant smile. My simple act has a profound purpose, which is for me to make a connection with each person in the room, so that there is a realisation that my thoughts and ideas are not just carried in the words I say, but in the relationships that I establish. I assure the audience that no one is invisible to me during my presentations. I am not just giving a talk; I am trying to inspire people to adopt a living philosophy and its practices.

I shy away from calling myself an 'inspirational speaker', because I have experienced sitting in audiences when speakers have used techniques and content to engage their audiences, but have not engaged with individuals at a personal level; thereby leaving them disempowered to really engage with the subject of their talk. Have you had similar experiences when you have felt 'missed' and left with the impression that the presenter has given the same talk umpteen times before?

I believe that deep learning occurs in the space between people, so authentic modelling of the process of being a values-based person is vital if the messages contained in my words are going to resonate with people who are just like you and me. When I was a schoolteacher, I soon realised that I might think I was teaching one lesson, but each student was hearing it differently and learning different things, because they were hearing my words through the filter of their own experience, upbringing and culture. It is the same for each person who reads this book: each individual will sense different meanings as my words interact with their life experiences.

Thus, this simple act of silent connection helps to establish the beginning of a relationship and intimacy. I have noticed that people who are genuinely interested in others, on initial meetings, take time to make eye contact and just *be present* for a few seconds before speaking. I remember being made extremely aware of this process when taking an active part in an education conference in Edinburgh. The principal guest was the Dalai Lama, who had this gift in abundance, and he made each new meeting very special for each of us. I would recommend that you make this a part of your awareness when you are meeting both friends and strangers. They will sense a pleasant difference in you.

Are you a people-watcher? I often turn a visit to my local supermarket into a rich experience of people-watching, especially of parents/carers with their children in tow. My observations have led me to the conclusion that if you want to learn about parenting in its many diverse forms, then watch as children are taken shopping. For instance, the parent with the misbehaving child, who is shouting and running amok in the aisles, and whom other shoppers are pretending to ignore, suddenly shouts out, 'Shut up you little brat. I'll tell your Dad when I get you home. You're really a nasty bit of work.' Or the parent you overhear saying, 'Now Jessica, where are the baked beans? It's spelt b-e-a-n-s. Ah yes, well done dear, you are clever.' Of course, these examples are caricatures, extremes, but they illustrate the range of parenting that makes up our society.

I would suggest that there are simple key skills/understandings about parenting that, if generally adopted, could transform relationships for the better in so many homes and classrooms. The central maxim to remember is that adults should never tell off *a child*, only (if appropriate) the *child's behaviour*. In the first example, the child is told that they are 'a nasty bit of work'. In hearing this, probably repeatedly, the child will develop an understanding that they are not liked for who they are. Subconsciously, they say to themselves, 'If I can't be noticed for being good, then I'll get attention by being bad.' Often they will carry this self-perception throughout life, because they have been thwarted in their efforts to cultivate a meaningful attachment with significant adults, such as their parents.

I think that we need to invest in finding ways of supporting the development of parenting skills across the whole of society. I remember talking with a secondary school teacher in Merthyr Tydfil (in South Wales), who pointed out to me that, in her community, they had children who had been parented by children, who had been parented by children, who had been parented by children – three generations! These individuals hadn't had the chance to develop many basic parenting skills, because they had been expected to raise their children alone and not as part of an extended family. Do you notice that, despite many examples to the contrary, there is a current lack of understanding about how to be an effective and loving parent? The teacher in Wales was not being unnecessarily critical – she loved the people in her community. However, she recognised that the community was no longer raising its children as it once did, when there was shared responsibility with grandparents, aunts, uncles and friends living locally, who passed on the wisdom of parenting and shared in that responsibility.

Without such cultural wisdom, we have, at one end of the spectrum, neglected and even abused children and, at the other end, over-indulged, potentially selfish children (demanding the latest iPad) who actually seek meaningful relationships, based on love and trust.

My intention is not to paint a picture of doom and gloom, because I am optimistic   as this book will show – that we can help and support all parents and adults in all societies to be at ease in the role of a parent/caregiver.

So, what do I hope that you will gain from reading this book? My main purpose is to inspire you to adopt universal, positive human values in your work and life and be a role model for them. I would like you to be so inspired that you will want to be an active part of a growing worldwide movement for transformational change. I hope that, as you take the journey with me through the pages of this book, you will conclude that the movement is not just an idealist's dream. You will gain the understanding needed to transform your own life and read the evidence about how values-based education (VbE) is transforming the lives of individuals and institutions, such as schools, and reaching out into all aspects of society.

One such school is Revoe (in Blackpool). Whenever I give a presentation about values-based education, I usually begin by showing a picture of a pupil at Revoe School. His name is Trev and I met him when I was invited to the school's 'Grand Opening of Parliament'. Revoe has moved on from the notion of a school council to ensuring that the children feel really involved in the leadership and management of the school (a key to how they have transformed pupil behaviour).

Firstly, a bit of background. A few years ago Revoe was judged by the English inspection service, Ofsted, to be a failing school; in fact, one of the worst in the country. It sits within what is described as a socially challenged catchment area. It was at this point that Cath Woodall was appointed to be the head teacher and began the task of transformation. On first meeting Cath, after a values presentation for Lancashire head teachers, I was aware that I was in the presence of an outstanding, optimistic leader with huge determination and the necessary practical skills to create a learning environment that would transform the school. She knew that, to provide a rich education for the pupils, she would need to embrace the community and demonstrate that Revoe was a good school. One of the first tasks was to ensure that the children came to school, so each morning she asked her teaching assistants to form a series of human buses. They would go out into the community and call at the children's homes to collect the pupils, who, for whatever reason, may have been reluctant to come to school. At first, the teaching assistants were met with a varied reception but, as the weeks passed, the community began to understand that Cath wanted the very best for their children, so they began to support her innovative initiatives.

Back to Trev. I spotted him by himself, waiting for the Parliament to begin. He seemed very glum, so I asked him if he was OK. He paused, eyeing me suspiciously, and then he said in a tearful voice, 'Mrs Woodall says that you are the important visitor who gives talks. My name is Trev; I'm in Year 4. You know, I am the Minister of Finance, but my Mum and Dad can't be bothered to come and see me today. They never come!' He then looked down at the ground and, for a moment, I considered what I could say that might be of some help. I then said, 'OK, can I be here for you? What's more, can I take your picture and, whenever I begin a talk, I will show your picture?' He glanced at me with a look that conveyed a mixture of hope and disbelief. We then went into the school's hall for the Grand Opening of Parliament, which was terrific, with all the staff and children entering into the spirit of the occasion. A wonderful moment was when Cath came in as the Queen to open Parliament – inducing a ripple of laughter from the parents and community members attending. Trev was great.

I have kept my promise to Trev and I have proved it to him because, some while ago, a professional development day was being held at the school by the National Education Trust (NET) and I had been asked to speak about the growing number of schools that are becoming values-based. Before I began, I asked Cath if Trev could be asked to come to the hall. He was now in Year 6. Without question she agreed and, with a broad smile, Trev arrived in the hall, and I invited him to sit at the front as I began my talk – with his smiling picture on the screen. I wish you could have seen the expression on Trev's face as it lit up with pride. Later, Cath confided in me that my two simple acts had done wonders to raise the self-esteem of this boy, who so desperately needed the approbation of adults. Healthy attachments and good relationships are the cornerstone of a values-based school.

Trev and Revoe School represent what I hope will be gained by people and organisations that adopt values-based education. In a nutshell, this is *inspiration* to want to be the best people that we can be, in our personal, family, community and work life. So, as I set out on the journey of writing this book, my purpose is to inspire you and to give you some important practical tools that will help you transform both your own life and the life of the school, business or company in which you work. Although the majority of my examples will be from my own background, which is in education, they can equally and effectively be applied to any business or institution – the core principles are the same.

How can you get the most from reading this book? May I make a few suggestions? Firstly, let me check: Do you know where your heart is?

Please take a moment to place one of your hands over your heart and just leave it there for a few seconds – can you feel your heart beating?

In so many countries now, young people are encouraged to think cognitively and apply deductive logic to problem-solving. We learn to use objective, scientific methods which we bring to our listening and reading. We are taught to break down argument and to be critical, looking for the flaws in reasoning. This is a great skill which I use myself, but I believe that we no longer have the correct balance between the cognitive and affective domains. By affective, I mean the area of feelings and emotions that fuel our creativity and help us to be fully integrated human beings. So, when reading this book, ask yourself how you *feel* about what you are reading, not just what you *think* about it. Maintain an open mind and sense what could help you to see the world through a different or adjusted lens; this will enhance your awareness and your consciousness.

Next, can you remain positive whilst you read this book? What is your mood at the moment?

Keep a check on yourself, as you will absorb more from my words if you are in a positive, relaxed state of mind. Research shows that children learn best when teaching is fuelled with positive emotion and when there is challenge, tempered with humour and fun.

Finally, are you a perfect person?

There was a man in an audience once, who, on hearing this question, put up his hand. I asked him why he thought he was perfect. His reply brought a roar of laughter when he said, 'I think I'm perfect, because my Mum says I am!' I don't know if he was saying this with his tongue in his cheek – I suspect that he was. The truth is that none of us have reached perfection. I know I haven't – my family and friends often remind me of my many flaws. The point is that talking about values can make some of us feel uncomfortable, because we are fully aware of our foibles. Please accept yourself for who you are today and join me on a lifetime's journey of self-improvement.

You are entitled to ask the question, 'Who is Neil Hawkes and what gives him the right to write a book with a focus on values?' Those who know me well will appreciate that I avoid the spotlight being turned on me, preferring instead to be a king-maker rather than a king. The reason for this is that I observe what happens when a person's ego takes control of them. It often causes people to cease being in touch with their innate human qualities and, instead, become deluded by power, wealth or fame. TV reality shows feed this appetite for what I term *false recognition*. *True recognition* is being valued and seen for who you really are, which I believe leads to people being comfortable in their own skin, as they shun the illusion of power and position. When asked the question, 'What do you do?' I am pleased to reply that I am proud to be a teacher. I have had the privilege of teaching people across all age groups. However, I currently focus my energy on teaching adults and young people about the benefits of basing their lives on a serious consideration of universal, positive human values.

I am indebted to Frances Farrer, whose wonderfully crafted and inspiring book, *A Quiet Revolution* (2000), told the story of many of the influences on my early life, as a student teacher, head teacher, local authority education adviser and then as the head teacher of West Kidlington School (in Oxfordshire). It was at West Kidlington that my career seemed to take on an incredible energy, as I was privileged to work with an exceptionally gifted group of teachers and support staff, who were supported by an enlightened governing body. The chair of governors, Bob Laines, a respected community leader, created a political and social environment that encouraged me to be an educational entrepreneur. For just under seven years, we all worked creatively together to harness the energy of the school's community to see if we could raise academic achievement and help the pupils to develop good character.

My leadership reflected my belief that the key role of a head teacher is to release the creative dynamic of all who work in the school. In an institution, such as a school or company, there should never be a hierarchy of relationships, only a hierarchy of roles. The outcome was that the adults willingly gave their time, talents and enthusiastic support to the life of the school. As people, we realised that we weren't values neutral because every time we spoke we revealed our intrinsic values to the pupils. After much discussion, we decided to introduce the pupils to a form of values education, the process of which I will describe in Chapter 6.

The Values Sculpture: West Kidlington School believes that the world in the future will be held up, or not, by the values that children develop when they are growing up. That is why the school is such an important part of this process. The sculptor Wendy Marshall inspired the children to think about how they could depict their values holding up the world. The hands and arms, modelled on the pupils' bodies, represent the five continents.

We soon found that this special focus on values made a profound difference, not only to the children, but on the adults too. West Kidlington School does not claim to have invented values education; a cursory investigation on the Internet will show that the subject has a rich and varied philosophical history spanning over two thousand years. What West Kidlington School can modestly claim is that it was one of the first schools, in modern times, to deliberately and systematically teach its pupils about positive human values, and where the adults consistently modelled them. Later in this book, I describe some of the other unique elements of West Kidlington's methodology and pedagogy. I am delighted that the practice is still embedded and enriched in the school, under the caring leadership of the school's current head teacher, Eugene Simmonds.

The word soon spread that school life was a bit different at West Kidlington. The principal education adviser for Oxfordshire, Richard Howard, gave his full support and the Ofsted inspection visit confirmed the school as very good with outstanding features. Visitors started coming from other parts of the world to see for themselves what was making this school unique. One was Professor Terence Lovat from Australia, who subsequently used the school as the blueprint for Australia's own development of values education. West Kidlington's reputation reached UNICEF headquarters in New York, and Cyril Dalais, head of the Early Childhood Education Cluster, invited Linda Heppenstall, the school's values coordinator, and me to join twenty other educators from around the world to plan an international values programme. From this meeting came the international values programme known as Living Values, which is now directed by a charity called ALIVE (Association of Living Values International). In the UK, head teachers and teachers visited the school. One regular visitor was Bridget Knight, who, when appointed as an adviser, took values education to schools in Herefordshire. Di Thomas, a head teacher from Bedfordshire, took the work to schools there.

Did everyone embrace the work? I mentioned Revoe School earlier and I remember two members of staff telling me that, when they first heard me talk about values work, they didn't think it would work in their school – it was 'too warm and fuzzy'. They admitted that they were completely cynical and could not see how it would work with children and a community that were, in their words, challenging. However, the head teacher encouraged them to give it their best go. I'm pleased to tell you that, when I recently met these teachers again, they said that they had been completely wrong and that it did work. In fact, it had changed their approach to teaching, which was now based on the principles of values-based education.

Another teacher, in a Bedfordshire middle school, had shared with me her scepticism about values education. However, she said that, over a five-year period, it had changed her life and her teaching. Before the current head teacher had introduced values education, she was often sick on her way to work because she found the job very stressful. Now she felt a renewed person, and her attitude to her pupils and teaching had changed completely, so that she now enjoyed coming to the school and had improved relationships with the pupils.

I hope these stories give you permission, if you need it, to read this book with healthy scepticism, because I think it is important for you to come freely to your own conclusions, and not feel that I am manipulating your thoughts and opinions in any way. I know, being a healthy sceptic myself, that it is only through personal experience and rigorous assessment that we can be sure of the validity of any claims that are made about values education.

This is why, whilst I was head teacher at West Kidlington, I decided to apply to Oxford University to study for a research doctorate. I was fortunate to be supervised by the former director of Oxford University's Department of Education, the acclaimed Professor Richard Pring, to whom I owe an enormous debt of gratitude. His intellectual insights, wide knowledge of education, wisdom and good humour sustained me over the nine years of my part-time research. My work was subjected to Richard's ongoing critical scrutiny, evaluated by members of the university and externally examined by Professor Bart McGettrick from Liverpool's Hope University. For this work, I was awarded the degree of Doctor of Philosophy (DPhil). The claims that were made in my own small-scale research were later endorsed by a large-scale research project, funded by the Australian government and conducted by Newcastle University (New South Wales) (Lovat et al., 2009). I will share some of these findings with you in Chapter 2.

In the following chapters, I will introduce you to what I am passionate about: what I think is the most important, exciting and inclusive philosophy, and related practices, which have the potential to ensure human sustainability and happiness in the twenty-first century. It is what I have termed the *philosophy of valuing: self, others and the environment*, better known as *values-based education*.

Some reflection points to ponder from this first chapter:

- Pause and take a minute or so to keep still and silent. In the silence, just explore what you have learned about what I find important in life. Then consider if this has made you reflect on your own priorities.

- Are you aware of your own thinking bias? For instance, do you like to focus on logical argument and concentrate on detail, or do you enjoy creative, big-picture thinking? Perhaps you are a person who achieves a balance between the two.

- What are the one or two main thoughts, feelings or sensations you have had whilst reading this chapter? Are you remaining in a positive frame of mind as you read this book? Remember that we gain the most from reading when we feel relaxed, purposeful and have a sense of enjoyment.

Chapter 2

Your values journey

In Chapter 1, I observed that no one can be values neutral. This is because life imbues us with values; we cannot escape from them. If you are a teacher, then your pupils will sense your values as soon as you speak to them. Likewise, if you are a parent or work in a shop, business or company, then your values will inform who you are, how you interact with others and out of which lens you see the world.

Your values journey …

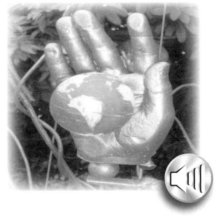

Let's reflect …

Take another pause now to reflect on your own values. Have you ever considered why you have them, where they came from and how you display them? If you could click on the speaker icon in the picture above, you would hear a version of 'Somewhere Over the Rainbow' by Israel Kamakawiwo'ole, from his album *Alone in IZ World*. My friend and sometimes co-presenter in Australia, psychologist Andrew Fuller of *Tricky Kids* fame, recommended it to me. Because of his amiable humour, I always think of him as the Billy Connolly of Oz. It is frequently helpful for some people, but not all, to have some appropriate music playing in the background as we are transported into our inner world of reflection. May I suggest that you now take some time, as much as you need, to reflect on your own values journey, and play your own music if it's practicable and desirable to do so.

Pause ...

I wonder what you have been thinking about? You may have been reflecting on your parents or other relations and how they gave you some of your values. I know that I absorbed many of mine from my paternal grandmother. She lived with my immediate family and spent a lot of time talking with me when I was a small child. I sometimes catch myself making judgements about how others are behaving, because Grandma was a stickler for good manners – the Victorian variety – and I now have to check that I don't form an inappropriate value judgement about another person because of Grandma's strong, clear voice, which I can still hear in my head. I suspect that you may have similar voices from your childhood.

You may have also reflected about teachers who taught you or, if you were inducted into a religion, the values you developed because of your beliefs. Your values may also have come from friends, especially during adolescence, when the influence of the peer group is very strong. The media, in all its forms, has also probably played a strong part in your choice of values. I often watch and listen to people talking together, and wonder if they chose particular values, which now guide their behaviour, or just absorbed them without being conscious about the process. I suspect that for most of us it is the latter. This is one of the reasons why I think that values have to be made explicit and brought fully into conscious awareness.

Look back at the picture of the globe in a golden hand. It is part of a values sculpture at Oatlands Infant School (in Surrey). Using symbols is a creative way of helping young children to learn about values. This hand, and there are many of them on the sculpture, was modelled on a child's hand. Can you guess which value the globe represents? There are no right or wrong answers because it depends on what you want it to represent. However, the school decided that this symbol of the world would represent the value of *unity*. Another hand has people holding hands fixed to it, representing cooperation.

Like yours, my own values journey spans my lifetime. In my introduction to Frances Farrer's *A Quiet Revolution* (2000), I acknowledged the profound influence of others on my own values development. These ranged from my grandmother, with her insistence on good manners, to the huge inspiration of Peter Long, head teacher of South Stoke Primary School (in Oxfordshire), during my final teaching practice. Such significant characters were profoundly influential on the development of my character. It was Peter's dedication and patience, when working with children, that helped me to understand the importance of establishing good relationships in schools; that quality education is about influencing the whole person, not merely about the transference of knowledge and skills. I watched Peter playing games with the children at break times, always giving freely of himself, enthusing pupils with his humour and inspiring them to be the best people that they could be. Peter became my role model, an educator I have kept in the forefront of my mind, especially when I have been in situations where people have not been able to model such positive values.

My values journey reached a very significant point when I was appointed head teacher of West Kidlington Primary and Nursery Schools (near Oxford). I'd had a very varied and fascinating career in education until this point. I had experienced two previous school headships and had been a local authority education adviser. Prior to coming to Kidlington, I had been the principal adviser of the Isle of Wight Education Service. It was here that I'd had an experience that changed the path of my career.

I clearly remember one September morning in a hotel in Shanklin. I was talking to a mixed group of teachers about what ingredients make a good school. All, I thought, was going well, until I noticed a female teacher in the back row of the audience, her arms folded, who seemed to be tutting under her breath. Being an experienced teacher, I automatically started to try to engage her, through eye contact and turning up the volume of my enthusiasm. None of my usual teaching techniques seemed to have any positive effect. In fact, she now seemed totally disengaged. It was then that I had my epiphany moment, because a voice in my head started to say to me: 'Neil, perhaps what she is thinking is, "What does he know about what he is talking about? If he really did know, he wouldn't just talk about it, *he would do it!*" ' In an instant, I realised what I needed to do. I stopped thinking of the disgruntled teacher and concentrated on the audience as a whole. Towards the end of my presentation, I noticed that she had unfolded her arms and was indeed smiling.

This didn't change my thinking though, because when I had finished the talk, I drove back to the county offices in Newport and saw John Williams, the chief officer, to tell him that I had decided to resign. He looked bemused. I explained to him how the teacher had acted as a catalyst, which had jolted me into realising that I wanted to put what I was telling others into practice. He was amazed. When I went on to say that I wanted to be a head teacher again, he tried to dissuade me, telling me that I would have a great future career as a chief education adviser/ officer in a large county.

My mind, however, was made up, so I looked in the situations vacant column of the *Times Education Supplement* (*TES*) and saw the following advertisement:

> Wanted,
> Head teacher,
> West Kidlington School
> just burned down!

I thought, 'Yes, this is the place for me, somewhere where I can build an innovative philosophy and practice, based on what I have been sharing with others.' Incidentally, the school had burned down on 5 November, Guy Fawkes or Bonfire Night in the UK, when someone had put a firework through the front door of the school and it had caught ablaze. The fire razed the school to the ground, except for the nursery, which the firefighters had managed to save. This was clearly a very sad time in the life of the school, as precious curriculum resources, as well as the school building, were lost in the fire. It was especially poignant as it happened only a few months before the school's much respected head teacher, Paul Canterbury, was due to retire. The advertisement for a new head teacher was calling out to me, so I applied. The rest is history because, when I was appointed to the school, I found that I had chosen (or had they chosen me?) a very special community of people.

The teaching and support staff gave me their full support, as did the governing body, chaired by Bob Laines. Whenever I talk about my values journey, I like to emphasise that the development of values education at the school was very much a corporate affair; I could not have led the process without the wonderful support of all the staff. I think I gained this partly because of my core beliefs as a leader. As I said in Chapter 1, I believed (and still do) that my core purpose was to provide the conditions that would release the dynamic creativity of all who worked in the school, so that they could give of their very best.

This meant that each employee would acknowledge the role they were playing in the school (e.g. office manager, teacher, teaching assistant, site manager), but this role did not mean that we were considered by each other as either better or worse as people – we were all equal. Too often schools, businesses and institutions are organised using a hierarchy of relationships – the boss is at the top of the staff photo display in the reception area and the person who cleans is at the bottom; the boss has his or her car park space near to the front door, others at a corresponding distance. I am sure that you can think of your own examples. In these settings, the new employee has to be silent and learn the culture of the organisation – and to acknowledge that the boss and senior leadership team have the best ideas. This is not how more enlightened organisations function and is far removed from a values-based one.

At West Kidlington, my predecessor, Paul Canterbury, had fostered an excellent team of caring, open-minded people who were skilled in whatever role they played in the school. It was on this strong foundation that I was able to build a values-based organisation. Frances Farrer asked if she could write an article about our work for the *TES*. She became more and more interested in the values concepts and, after writing another article for the *TES*, she suggested a book. Random House published *A Quiet Revolution* over ten years ago and it has made its way into several other countries, including Pakistan and the United States. I cannot overstate what a masterpiece this book is, as Frances captured the very soul of the school in her writing.

For just under seven years, the school worked to embed values education in the curriculum. We developed our own resources, but also used other excellent materials produced by organisations such as the Human Values Foundation. We wanted to celebrate our success in embedding values education and make a statement about it to the community. To this end, we asked Wendy Marshall, a professional sculptor, to work with Year 6 pupils (11-year-olds) to design and create a sculpture that reflected our values philosophy (this is the photo that appears in Chapter 1). It turned out to be an inspiration for all. The children suggested that there should be five arms to represent the children of the five continents of the world. The arms hold up the world, which is an inspirational metaphor implying that, in the future, it will be the positive values of the children that will raise up our world.

Without wishing to sound grandiose, I do believe that the future of communities, countries and, yes, humanity is dependent on the values that our children develop, which will guide their thoughts and actions as adults. The school community of West Kidlington did not invent values education; what I think is unique is its claim to have been the first school to explicitly and deliberately embed the philosophy and practices of values-based education in every aspect of its life and work over an extended period of time. In fact, the school is still attracting

visitors because the work has become so embedded in the consciousness of staff at the school. It is they who saw the benefits of the
approach and have subsequently inducted two head teachers into its
methods. The current head, Eugene Symonds, enthusiastically
embraces the concept:

> Leading the school, where values-based education all started, is
> both a privilege and intensely humbling in equal measure. It is a
> privilege to be part of school where so many members of our
> learning community share my commitment to the values of com-
> passion, care, creativity, courage and cooperation. It is also
> deeply humbling to see the impact these values have on our
> children's achievements. Headship can be a relentlessly chal-
> lenging job, but I am proud to be associated with such a uniquely
> enriching place of learning.

Eugene has skilfully led the school with great tenacity, keeping the
values dynamic alive and fresh, ably assisted by his incredible
Liverpudlian humour.

During my headship, I clearly remember one particular visitor to the
school, Bridget Knight, who at that time was the deputy head of
another local school in Kidlington. She had heard about the values
work and asked if she could come to a school assembly and talk to me
afterwards about the benefits and challenges of becoming a values-
based school. I remember Bridget light up when she saw what we were
doing. She later gained her own headship and developed an outstanding school at Stonesfield (in Oxfordshire). She went on to be a schools
adviser in Herefordshire, where she motivated head teachers to turn
their schools into values-based schools. The quiet revolution of West
Kidlington spread and was gaining momentum. After a presentation to
Bedfordshire head teachers, Di Thomas, head of Greenfield Lower
School, was similarly convinced and became the focus for nurturing
values schools across the county. Similar stories can be told in Surrey
and other parts of the UK.

I decided to focus my energies on working with head teachers and
school communities so that we could build up a movement that could

show the positive effects of adopting values education. I consciously shied away from trying to convince politicians and others in authority, because I had found that such people tend to want very fast results. I also believed that it was important for teachers to really believe in the work and not think that it was an official requirement from above. I recall that Bridget Knight and I were invited to see an official, who warmly received us at 10 Downing Street, in the last days of Tony Blair's government. We were informed that it was too late for values education to become an initiative (as it had in Australia) and that we should perhaps return when a new government was appointed. I am not sorry about that, because there is now much more genuine interest as we are able to show the effects and benefits of values-based education across more schools.

Australia was a different story. Professor Terence Lovat (Emeritus Professor, University of Newcastle (Australia) and Senior Research Fellow, University of Oxford) was excited about values education. He thought that West Kidlington's experience of values-based education should become the gold standard for Australia's comprehensive values education initiative. Terry was one of a number of individuals who worked behind the scenes to convince politicians and educationists to support and invest in values education. A federal programme resulted which led to Australia spending upwards of $40 million dollars implementing values education in its schools. This was a very clever mixture of government initiative and local community support. Terry believes, as I do, that values-based education improves academic attainment whilst giving students the personal, social and moral skills to be global citizens. Terry says:

> As educational systems everywhere search for ways of improving academic achievement levels for all students, as well as preparing them with the personal, social, emotional and moral skills required for life in global societies, the credentials of values-based education are without peer. Evidence has shown that VbE has unusual potential to achieve all these goals at one and the same time. It fits well with the latest brain research that shows the interdependence of the thinking and feeling hemi-

spheres of the brain. It also fits well with all that we have learned about the effects of quality teaching and holistic pedagogy. VbE has the potential to combine the best of contemporary theory and practice about ways to optimize learning in the modern classroom.

Over the last ten years, I have had the privilege of supporting the wonderful team of values educators in Australia, speaking at conferences and schools across most states. Later in this chapter I will refer to the wealth of research from Australia that shows the impact of a systematic development of values education.

As I write, I suspect that you may now be wondering if everyone has cheered with support for values-based education. What about the sceptics? Surely some have thought it a waste of time, and not really effective in raising standards and improving character and behaviour? As I observed in Chapter 1, on a visit to a Bedfordshire Middle School, I met an experienced teacher who shared with me how she had been very sceptical about the potential benefits of values education. I asked her to tell me what affect values education has had on her experience as a teacher. She paused, took a deep breath and replied:

OK, I had taught here for eleven years and, up to the time that the current head teacher was appointed, I'd had a pretty rotten time of it. At my professional interview, he asked me what I thought of the school. I told him that the sight of a red jumper made me physically sick on my way to school. I loathed coming; I hated being here. I was probably the biggest sceptic of anybody about how values education could possibly turn anything around. I just couldn't see it. Gradually, I saw that things were changing. I was thinking more about the values and the pupils, in turn, were reflecting on them and, in a nutshell, I can't believe how my life, my approach to children and teaching has changed in the last five years. There have been dramatic changes. I look back and I can't recognise that person, the life that I was leading and those relationships I had, or rather didn't have, with the children I was teaching.

This teacher's values journey gives a clear example of what so many parents and teachers have described about the intrinsic power of adopting what on the surface seems very simple, yet has profound consequences. I am often asked, frequently by politicians: 'What you say sounds wonderfully idealistic, but where is the research evidence to support your claims?' I actually agree with the underlying question, because I think it is important that the development of educational practice is grounded in sound research evidence. My impression is that, too often, educational policy is formed on ideological whims rather than in a consultative process that includes a considered analysis of research. Therefore, I think it is important that, without going into too much detail, I end this chapter by giving you the opportunity to reflect on the impressive research evidence.

Uniquely, in 2002, the Australian government made a concerted effort to fund and foster a range of activities to support schools in developing explicit, informed, systematic and effective approaches to values education in all areas of school policy and classroom practice. Values education is seen as a means of nurturing Australia's common democratic way of life, which includes equality, freedom and the rule of law. Values education has been supported throughout the country by schools and communities who have been keen to address values education from a community perspective. Values education and student well-being are now an integral part of Australian schooling, as they are seen as central to fostering high academic standards in the context of an ethically based school community.

I was delighted to have played a small part in this process, having been invited to be a keynote speaker at two National Values Education Forums. I remember flying into Australia from the UK for the first of these, my first trip down under, and not having planned to give myself sufficient time to get over the jetlag. I arrived in Canberra and found myself giving the keynote in what was for me the middle of the night. I was so sleepy, I recall thinking that I was hallucinating as I gave my talk, but I discovered afterwards that only I had been aware of this and a very tuned-in audience of empathetic values educators had rapturously received my ideas (and jokes).

The Australians used my practical experience and research as a former head teacher, who had implemented values education in a UK school, to underpin the professional development materials for their teachers. I have made seven subsequent visits to Australia to share good practice and to inspire school communities to scaffold everything they do with positive human values, such as respect, integrity, responsibility and compassion. My own research at Oxford University, which I completed in 2005, made a number of tentative claims regarding the contribution that values education can make to quality education. I am delighted that these have now been validated by a large-scale action research project in Australia (Lovat et al., 2009). The Australian research, which was an integral part of the National Framework for Values Education in Australian schools (Commonwealth of Australia, 2005), revealed the following five key interrelated impacts of values education:

1   Values consciousness

2   Well-being

3   Agency

4   Connectedness

5   Transformation

These five identified impacts support my assertion that a systematic and planned approach to values education can improve students' engagement with schooling, promote better learning outcomes and enhance students' social and emotional well-being. The evidence conclusively shows how values education can transform classrooms, relationships, school environments, teachers' professional practice and parents' engagement in their children's schooling. I hope you will be fascinated by the following brief outline of the impacts, which have provided rich evidence to support my belief that values education should be at the heart of all individuals, communities and organisations.

Impact 1: Values consciousness

It was found that deliberate and systematic values education enhances values consciousness. For instance, students, teachers and parents developed an increased consciousness about the meaning of values and the power of values education to transform learning and life. Encouraging the skill of reflection is crucial to this process. Such increased awareness resulted in more than a superficial understanding of values but was related to a positive change in student behaviour. Incredibly, teachers began to think more deeply about their teaching and the values that they modelled, both in and outside the classroom. Students reported on how values consciousness had impacted on their actions, which had become more altruistic.

It was discovered that the establishment of communication about values between teachers, students and parents, through newsletters, community forums and artistic performances, had very positive effects. For instance, giving time and space for teachers and parents to be involved in their children's values education both enhanced relationships and afforded time for parents to reflect on their own values.

Impact 2: Well-being

Students' well-being was enhanced through the application of values-focused and student-centred teaching, which gave time for them to reflect deeply on the nature of values, and what these meant to them and others. Teaching strategies included silent sitting, reflective writing, multimedia production, drama performances and poetry writing. In thinking about, acting on and feeling values, students developed awareness of self-worth, empathy and responsible personal behaviour. I was delighted that evidence from the data showed that values education had a very positive effect on the sense of self of students who are 'at risk', marginalised or disadvantaged.

Students also developed a greater understanding of the impact of their actions on the well-being of others. Values education helped students and teachers to look inside themselves, and really work out what they value and who they are. There was compelling evidence that well-being impacts were experienced by teachers, parents and families, and in classroom and whole-school environments.

Impact 3: Agency

Agency is at first sight a strange term. It stands for the capacity of individuals to act independently and to make choices and act on them – to be self-disciplined. The evidence showed that values education strengthened student agency when it involved various forms of giving, outreach and working in the community; for instance, through values action projects that allowed students to enact their values, such as thinking about how the school could more actively support a residential care home for the elderly. Agency was developed through meaningful, real-life experiential learning, such as engagement in community projects – where there was opportunity for the development of student voice, initiative and leadership – and an explicit focus on ethical, intercultural and social issues.

Structured reflection on their experiences and learning was a central element in developing agency. Such activity generated a deep sense of 'self' and 'others'. For values learning to take place, activities have to be deeply personal, deeply real and deeply engaging. Not surprisingly, relationships between students and teachers were enhanced through such activities. I believe that this research finding has wide implications for teacher agency and teacher education, in terms of understanding how to teach and structure learning in the context of an active enquiry-based curriculum.

Impact 4: Connectedness

The research showed how values education builds positive and wide-ranging connections between teachers, students and parents. It supported student engagement in learning, improved parent engagement in their children's learning, and allowed teachers to develop new relationships with their students and each other, and the parents and families in their school community. This was achieved through shared goals and practices in values education, which led to the development of mutual feelings of respect, trust and safety, and varied opportunities for collaboration. The research findings show that the values led to improved and stronger relationships between teachers, students and parents; for example, more respectful behaviours in the classroom, school and home. Community engagement brought about quality outcomes for teachers, students and parents.

Impact 5: Transformation

I am sure that it won't come as a surprise that change and transformation was at the heart of the values projects. It was the result of teachers and students being urged to engage in continuous reflection on the actions they implemented in their schools. Key changes were in modifications in professional practice, as well as personal attitudes, behaviours, relationships and group dynamics. Transformations – for instance, in the development of getting on well together (relational trust) – were experienced and observed by teachers, students and parents alike. Also, the ability of students to concentrate in their lessons (academic diligence) was enhanced, leading to greater academic achievement.

The data point to profound transformations in student learning. Students developed a deeper understanding of complex issues; for example, how to understand sophisticated concepts about values when these are explicitly taught. Such teaching changed their attitude and perception of a value, which led to a positive change in their behaviour. Students and parents experienced personal change and reported seeing changes in others. For instance, a student said how the class had positively evolved and that values had helped them to become more mature, adjusted people. The research showed the profound professional and personal transformation that can result when the parent community is involved in students' learning.

So what does this tell us?

I hope you can now understand why I am so passionate about the impacts of values education. The research evidence is such an important part of the international values journey, as it shows the impact that values education has on encouraging quality education and parent/community involvement. It provides a sound rationale for parents, teachers and educational systems to recognise the importance of adopting values education. The National Framework for Values Education in Australian Schools has provided an important part of my personal values journey and matured my vision for the development of values-based schools. It provides the platform for the next chapter that answers one of the questions you may be asking: What is the starting point for values-based education?

Some reflection points to ponder from this chapter:

- Were you fascinated as you reflected on your own values journey and the impact it is having on your life?

- Are you sensing any differences between your personal and professional values journey? If so, what are they? What are the consequences of these differences?

● I would like to suggest that you keep a journal in which you can record your thoughts about this book and the impact it is having on you. It could form the basis of a new habit that will help you to consider and nurture your life as your values journey develops in the future.

● As a parent, teacher or in another role, collect evidence about the effects that having a greater values awareness is having on your life. Please share this with others and, if you come up with some new evidence, please let me know at www.valuesbasededucation.com.

Chapter 3

What is the starting point for values-based education?

This lovely picture of a Swedish pre-school prompts me to think about the starting point for values-based education. I would like to ask you a question, and I want you to answer intuitively, quickly and speak your truth. There isn't a right answer. If your answer to the question is yes, then put your hand up and wave it in the air. If your answer is no, then leave your hand down. So here's the question: Are you wonderful? Decided? I wonder where your hand is? Thanks, you can return to your normal position now. I am curious about what you thought and felt when I asked you the question and on what basis you either raised your hand or left it down.

I have been asking this illuminating question of audiences in many different countries and I am fascinated by what I have found. For instance, the majority of Scandinavians raise their hand. When I ask them why, they make remarks like, 'I am a unique person like everyone is', 'It is so wonderful that I am having this experience in the world' or 'I am wonderful because I have been given so many blessings'.

This is in stark contrast to the reaction I so often get in the UK, when usually only a minority raise their hands. In Australia and New Zealand about seventy-five per cent of hands are raised and in parts of America two hundred per cent: each person puts up two hands! I can only speculate at the cultural reasons for these differences and I'm sure that you will have your own view too. Maybe the British associate being wonderful with 'showing off'. Perhaps they denigrate themselves or possibly it may show an underlying poor self-image. One person suggested to me that teachers don't think that they are wonderful because they have suffered from such a negative image, fuelled by politicians and the media.

My hope is that, if you are someone who feels reluctant to say that you are wonderful, by the end of this book you will have reconsidered and recognise yourself as truly wonderful. If you ever feel that your self-image needs a boost, then stand in front of a mirror, raise both arms and adopt a 'hero' pose and shout, 'WOW!' I find this really does do wonders! More seriously: Why do I think you *are* wonderful? I think that you are wonderful because you send messages to the future. If you are a parent or a teacher, children are watching you and listening to you. You are helping to form them as human beings. You are moulding their personality, attitudes, behaviours and dispositions. Your influence cannot be underestimated. In my view, the profession of teaching is so important in the development of a civilised, democratic society that it therefore should be respected and appropriately nurtured.

Older teachers often tell me how former pupils greet them in the street – frequently the ones that they had challenged in some way. I too remember being tapped on the shoulder as I was walking along a street in Swindon, where I had taught as a newly qualified teacher. I looked round and up at a tall man who was beaming down at me. He said, 'Do you remember me?' I certainly did, how could I not remember Ferat! In a flash, I recalled my first day at the school and walking into a classroom to see Ferat tumbling on the floor with another lad. On entering the room, I remember him stopping and giving me a withering, disrespectful look. I recollect thinking, 'It's either going to be him or me that's going to control this class'; it turned out to be me.

After Ferat had got my attention he said, 'Yes, I bet you remember me! However, I just want to say a big thank you for what you did for me. My childhood was a difficult one in so many ways, but you didn't give up on me. I realise that who I am today is in no small way due to your patience and determination. I often think of you when I am dealing with other people and think, what would Mr Hawkes do?' He then shook my hand, gave me another beaming smile and walked on. These are the moments that make the job of a teacher, youth worker and parent so rewarding, when we realise how we influence the development of children, and help to form who they will be as adults. We do indeed send messages to the future!

The sentiment contained in the story of Ferat reminds me in some way of a special time I had with one of my grandchildren, Bertie, who was just about to start school. I was visiting the family and had woken early in the morning, so I headed for the kitchen to make a morning tea and have a few quiet moments before everyone else got up. To do this, I had to walk along a hallway past Bertie's bedroom and down some creaky stairs. I crept silently until I reached the stairs and made my way down. About halfway down, I was conscious of a presence and then I heard a small voice saying, 'Grandpa, Grandpa, will you play?' For a moment I wrestled with my values (what about my quiet cup of tea?) and then replied, 'Hi Bertie. Yes, let's play.' He wanted to get out his car collection and we proceeded to play as only boys can: few words, some sounds and quite a lot of action. Suddenly he stopped, looked at me with a very puzzled look and asked, 'Grandpa, why do I have to go to school?'

Have you ever asked yourself that question? I wonder what reply you would have given Bertie? We spent the next few minutes talking about all the interesting things he would be doing at school, which I knew to be an engaging, dynamic school. I think Bertie's question is a profound one and is central to any discussion about values-based education. So I think it would be helpful if I ask you to consider the following question for a few moments: What is the purpose of education?

Pause ...

I remember asking this question of a large, lively audience in Brisbane when a guy shouted from the back of the hall, 'Hey mate, I know what education is – it's a form of bloody social control!' I wonder what you think? Some people consider it is about passing on the knowledge and skills to pass examinations, others to prepare children for life, and some think it is to ensure that the economy of the country thrives.

I believe that the purpose of education is about the *flourishing of humanity*. I first heard this poetic expression when I listened to an engaging talk by Professor Bart McGettrick, from Liverpool's Hope University, and remember thinking, yes, that is the purpose of education. Bart inspired me to think about the differences between education and schooling, and whether schools actually do focus on helping children to flourish. I think children thrive when they are in values-based families and schools – for reasons I will explain later in this book.

How do we ensure that each person flourishes? What should be the focus of education? Again, Bart's words come immediately to mind: 'Education is a conversation, a conversation between generations about matters of significance.' It is about how we learn about our culture, our past and become excited about our future. It is between generations, because although the young learn from older people, older people can also learn from the young. For instance, I continue to be educated about technology, such as my iPhone, by my granddaughter, Alice, who has developed an understanding, speed and dexterity of which I am in awe.

My point is that we must have good relationships in order to have meaningful conversations that inspire us to embed learning and enable us to flourish as human beings. If you cast your mind back to the people who influenced you when you were young, I suspect they were individuals with whom you felt safe, connected and who you liked. I understand that young people often choose their exam preferences based on the relationships they have, or don't have, with their teachers. I wonder if this resonates with your experience?

The question that I hope is forming in your mind is this: Why then do we need values education? In order to consider this question, I would like to invite you to take a few moments to think about the values of society. From your own experience, what values dominate your society?

Pause ...

I recently asked an audience in Luton this question. There were a range of answers, from too much focus on consumerism, materialism, money, instant fame, personality cults and greed, to expressions of individual and group altruism and compassion. Of course, we can consider the many examples of people acting selflessly for the good of society. Generally though, members of the Luton audience, who from my experience were typical in their reactions, thought that society was caught up in a mood of selfishness. Evidence to support such views can be seen in the media. Consider the example from a tabloid newspaper with the headline, 'Nasty not nice'. The article suggested that reality shows have high audience ratings when the judges are sarcastic and aggressive. It gave an example of one talent show that was losing in the ratings war against another popular reality show, so the judges were told by the show's producers to up the ante!

On an even more serious note, questions may be asked about the values in a society when there are riots. I remember some members of an Enfield audience becoming very angry when I showed a slide of a young person taking part in the London riots of 2011. They argued that members of their community were being vilified by politicians and the media without stopping to ask deeper questions about the social environment that create the conditions that lead to such rioting.

One woman shouted at me, 'Do you know that all the youth clubs were closed in our area and the kids have little to do?'

Such views exemplify the passions that individuals and communities feel about issues of equality and fairness in societies around the world. These were summed up in Richard Wilkinson and Kate Pickett's book *The Spirit Level* (2009), which looked at inequalities between nations. Few of us though appear to ask questions about the social circumstances that lead to communities rioting. Similar thoughts have been expressed to me in Australia, the Netherlands, New Zealand, Singapore, Sweden and the United States, where people claim that they feel under pressure from an excessive emphasis on consumerism. It seems paradoxical that, as individuals, we do not want what collectively we are creating. Such dilemmas create feelings of powerlessness.

In considering such issues, the Children's Society in the UK issued a landmark report entitled, *A Good Childhood, Searching for Values in a Competitive Age* (Leyard and Dunne, 2009). This report considered what currently constitutes childhood and found that it is dominated by the so-called 'me' culture – excessive individualism and making the most of your own life rather than contributing to the good of others. It looked at how society can develop a more caring ethic. It concurred with the views of my audiences that the values of generosity and fairness are more difficult to inculcate when we are told that we need more material goods and to compete successfully against others.

The report is full of positive suggestions about how to enable children to have a good childhood. For instance, it refers to the importance of the values work of West Kidlington School and its positive effect on well-being, particularly the development of children's capacity to adopt a moral code of behaviour by focusing on a values vocabulary. I will be explaining how this is achieved in Chapter 10. Drawing on the evidence of discussions I have had with audiences around the world, I am convinced that we need to empower individuals to consider the words of Gandhi who invited people to be the change that they wanted to see in the world.

Three such people are Eric, Hans and Max in the Netherlands. A few years ago, they were impressed with the message of the values philosophy and practice after I gave a presentation at a European conference for school principals in Cyprus. For two years, they worked to convince their colleagues in Helmond that all teachers there should hear the message. They made an ambitious plan, which included erecting a huge tent that would accommodate a thousand teachers, and invited me to inspire the teachers and support staff to embrace values-based education. My wife, Jane, who has been a driving force in the development of what we have termed 'the inner curriculum' (more on this in Chapter 8), joined me during this humbling, incredible experience, which was brought about by the vision and determination of three wonderful values-driven people.

The values philosophy empowers children and adults to take personal responsibility for their thoughts and actions. This is exemplified in schools as diverse as Sancta Maria College (New Zealand), Chantry School (UK), St Charles Boremeo School (Australia), the Hornbill School (Brunei) and so many others that I have been privileged to visit around the world. These schools are leading a movement for cultural change and helping children to use their positive values to become the best possible people that they can be. They are an integral part of an exciting philosophical tradition that we will consider in the next chapter.

Some reflection points to ponder from this chapter:

- Having read this chapter, do you understand why you are wonderful? Please consider re-reading the beginning of this chapter again if you are unsure.

- What will you do today and this week to boost your self-belief? A daily mantra can help, such as, 'Every day, in every way, I'm getting better and better!'

● If you have influence over children, how are you helping them to flourish? What practical steps can you take to help them? One parent told me that he was going to spend more time actively listening to his child.

● During today, be aware of the children you see or meet and consider what sort of childhood they are having. Are they being helped to be socially aware and concerned about the needs of others? What can you do to contribute to a *good* childhood?

Chapter 4

The philosophy of values-based education

> Isn't it the moment of most profound doubt that gives birth to new certainties? Perhaps hopelessness is the very soil that nourishes human hope; perhaps one could never find sense in life without first experiencing its absurdity.
>
> Václav Havel

Havel's words remind me of a challenging time several years ago, a low point in my personal life, when I found solace and a safe haven while visiting my close friends Alan and Sally Burn for the New Year's holiday. I was reflecting on the direction of my life's journey and decided to read a little book that I had picked up at a local bookshop – *Man's Search for Meaning* by Victor Frankl. I remember snuggling down in bed with the wind howling outside and I stared at the cover. For a moment, I felt a shudder down my spine and I wondered if this really was the book I wanted to read. The barbed wire illustration made my heart sink. Nevertheless, something inside me, my intuition, convinced me to continue. Some time later, I glanced at the clock in the bedroom and found that three hours had flown by, as I had been gripped by Frankl's profound, life-changing account, which I now recommend should be read by everyone.

At the beginning of the Second World War, Frankl, a Jew, had been told by his father to go the United States, where he had won a scholarship to study psychiatry, as conditions in his native Austria were becoming so difficult for them and he would be safer abroad. Victor refused, saying that he wished to remain with his parents. That decision soon cost him his freedom, because he became one of the millions who were taken on cattle trucks to concentration camps. After a treacherous journey, he found himself facing an SS officer on the unloading ramp at Auschwitz. He sensed that this was a selection process, one that he passed, as the officer's fingers did not indicate that he should take the way to the gas chambers but, instead, to a living hell as a slave worker. Frankl, unlike most of his family and millions of others, survived the experience of life in concentration camps.

Whilst he was living out his existence in the camp, he kept his mind active by observing human behaviour in the most degraded of circumstances. For instance, he wondered why two people could enter Auschwitz, who were similar in terms of health, background and age, but, after only a few weeks, one would lie down at night, their spirit extinguished, and die, whilst the other continued to struggle for existence. What do some people have that makes them survivors? Frankl argued that it is the person who has a *meaning* and *purpose* in their life who has the spark that keeps them wanting to live. Perhaps it is the family with whom they want to be reunited or the doctoral thesis that they want published. He also observed that, when everything is taken away from the prisoner and he is standing in rags with just a camp number tattooed on an arm as his identity, he still has one freedom left to him. Can you think what that freedom is? It was the freedom to choose his attitude, because no one could control his thoughts.

I think that these two profound insights are at the very heart of a values-based family, school or other organisation: the search for meaning and purpose, and the freedom to choose your attitude. Frankl's words fed my spirit, and his message of hope rekindled my belief in the potential of humanity and the vital importance of nurturing values-based education in all aspects of life.

After the war, Frankl was aware that for many young people there was an existential vacuum, but, on questioning young people, he found that the majority were not looking for money or riches, but for a meaning and purpose in their lives to fill the void. I have observed city life late in the evening and noticed how many people are in search of happiness through excessive alcohol, drugs and inappropriate sexual behaviour. It seems that when we don't have meaning and purpose in our lives, we grasp at superficial quick fixes that, on waking the next day, leave us with a feeling of emptiness, because the very soul of our human being has not been nourished. A values-based family and school gives opportunities for children to find their meaning and purpose, and helps them to sense and shape their future. They encourage children to understand that their values have to be consistent with their purpose and define the way that they try to achieve this.

In one of his lectures after the war, Frankl explained that, although he was getting old, he was taking flying lessons. His instructor had told him that if he wanted to fly to an airport that was in a straight line from his starting point, but there was a cross wind, then he would have to fly north of the airfield in order to end up where he wanted to be. He suggested that this was a metaphor for how we should view human beings: if we see someone as he is, then we make him worse, but if we overestimate him, then we promote him to what he could be. Therefore, we have to see people's potential, and we need to be idealists in order to be realists. Frankl's thinking was based on a maxim of the philosopher Goethe, who said: 'If we treat people as they are, we make them worse. If we treat people as they ought to be, we help them become what they are capable of becoming.'

It is therefore my contention that each of us should try to see the true potential in others, taking care not to create limits for them by our own inappropriate or inaccurate perceptions of their capabilities. I have always owned up to being an optimistic idealist, because I believe that this is the best platform from which, as a teacher, I can help others to realise their potential. Many of the teachers I have been privileged to observe have had this trait in their character, which can be nurtured in a values-based school or other setting. People who don't know me may conclude that I am unrealistic. However, like most of us, my life story has regularly presented challenges. These experiences have given me the opportunity to develop aspects of my character such as determination and perseverance. Therefore, I don't want to imply that being an idealist means that I don't recognise that normal human behaviour can be driven by thoughts and feelings that are far from altruistic. When we are stressed by events in our lives, our thoughts and feelings are frequently catapulted back to survival instincts, and our capacity to care for others and ourselves may be impaired. For instance, I am aware that if we have issues concerning our relationships or lack a secure sense of self, then we can be consumed with fearful thoughts and feelings.

Fear is a potentially limiting value and feeds behaviour that emanates from the limbic and reptilian parts of our brain. When we touch these aspects of our humanity, then our behaviours, if left unchecked, may be far from kind and rational. How often have you wondered why you did or said something that you now regret? In certain moments of intensity, any of us can experience this loss of control and touch what is sometimes referred to as the 'shadow side of humanity'. Fear and other limiting values can be the catalysts that spawn our selfish behaviour. Such egocentric conduct feeds our shadow side – most of us have one. I believe that it is only by recognising the potentially devastating effects of our shadow side that we can be mindful about behaving inappropriately. You will discover in this book that values-based education provides tools to help dissolve our shadow and to nurture the positive side of our humanity.

Try this experiment: get a jar with a screw lid, put some fleas in it and leave them for a few days. You will notice that the fleas will jump up to the lid and fall. After a week or so, unscrew the lid and see what happens. You will observe that the fleas jump up to where the lid was and no further. This is a metaphor that is also true for children. If our expectations are low, tainted perhaps by our limiting experiences or low expectations of ourselves, then the child will be limited too and perform down to low expectations. However, if our expectations are high, then we allow the child to achieve and have a positive sense of self. This unassuming yet profound thinking underpins the philosophy and practices that values-based families and schools put into practice.

On the other hand, I recall waiting to see a parent on a school open evening and watching her approaching me with her son in tow. Her opening words were, 'Well, I don't suppose he's any good at maths, because I wasn't!' In one sentence she was undoing all the work that I had been doing to raise her son's confidence. She later attended a parenting nurture group that I had organised, which gave me the opportunity to explain the importance of being positive with our children and how we can inadvertently create a limiting mindset.

During my education workshops, I often ask participants to think about their ideal classroom and ask themselves what ingredients would make it the best in the world. This question can equally be adapted to apply to home life. It always fascinates me why we do the things we do. I think that teachers teach the way they do partly because they remember how they were taught. Also, they absorb the practices that they learn in training and during teaching practice. Increasingly, I wonder if trainee teachers have the opportunity to consider the philosophical traditions that underpin good educational practices. If you are a teacher I would like to ask you: Whose philosophy underpins what you do in your classroom?

In helping you to answer this question, I would suggest that, if you have access to the Internet, you take a little time at the end of this chapter to search for more information about the lives of four people who have impacted on the way education has developed and who have profoundly affected my own thinking, of course along with many others. They are Aristotle, Maria Montessori, Martin Buber and Nel Noddings. So, what is the significance of these philosophers?

The great Greek philosopher, Aristotle (384–322 BC), developed ideas about children's moral education. He argued that children should be taught to act morally and then, as they matured, they would be able to understand because their actions would be based on sound moral principles. It is fascinating that his two aims for education were the development of intellectual capacities and moral education – the current outcome of a values-based school. Aristotle gave his curriculum a prescribed purpose: the pursuit of happiness. He believed that each person is motivated by the desire for long-term happiness and that the teacher's role is to help in the development of the pupil's mind by assisting in the establishment of an understanding of the real world. Happiness can be achieved through a process of contemplation, leading to intellectual understanding. This contemplative, reflective practice links Aristotle with Eastern mystics, who considered contemplation to be a profound practice and potentially the most important human activity.

Values-based education in the twenty-first century has adopted this rationale for the development of moral education. The active guidance by parents and teachers that enabled the pupil to become *just*, by performing *just acts*, was key to Aristotle's model for education. He assumed that parents had sufficient understanding to be engaged in the early stages of moral development. He reasoned that beginning with the development of moral habits would lead to the habit of doing things right. Thus, Aristotelian thinking about moral education is arguably the foundation on which the theory of values-based education is being built, with its emphasis on reflection, active discussion and practice of positive values words, such as respect, cooperation and tolerance.

I am now going to make a huge jump in time to the life of Maria Montessori (1870–1952). Maria challenged the thought that drew distinctions between the worlds of home, school and community. No one before her had argued that school should replicate aspects of the ideal home. School had been seen (and, to a large extent, still is today) as a bridge between home and community, socialising the child into cultural norms. There is an implied assumption that the child's home is a natural environment that functions appropriately for the nurturing of the child prior to attending school. Good parenting is assumed and little help is given to prepare people for carrying out the range of tasks associated with the role.

Montessori questioned the assumption that school is a bridge between home and community. She expounded the theory and practice of the *Casa dei Bambini* (the Children's Home or House). She argued that, for there to be peace in society, children need to be educated in a process where home, school and society are seen as continuous. Schools today are generally conceived as places to induct children into the dominant cultural norms of society – one based largely on continuous economic growth. Montessori wanted each school to represent the model of an ideal family, and the school environment to be safe, secure and loving, thereby encouraging the development of the right character. She maintained that putting children in the wrong environment would lead to abnormal development – dysfunctional adults. A values-based school takes seriously the development of an environment that promotes the conditions that create a calm and purposeful ethos, one that promotes excellence in all its forms.

Montessori's educational philosophy sympathetically resonates with my third philosopher, her contemporary Martin Buber. Throughout his life, Martin Buber (1878–1965) was deeply affected by the impact of his mother leaving him when he was only three years old. As a consequence of this experience, he later coined the expression *vergegnung* (mismeeting) to represent the failure to create a real meeting between people. He devoted his life to exploring how real meetings can be achieved. He described two types of relationships: *Ich-Du* (I-Thou) and *Ich-Es* (I-It). Throughout life, we can choose which of these relationships to have. The I-Thou relationship Buber described exists when participants are fully involved in a situation, whereas the I-It relationship is functional, automatic and allows us to negotiate our daily existence. In order to enter into I-Thou relationships, we must cultivate a sense of being present and allow the authentic self to sense the experience. This gives the individual the feeling of being really alive.

Buber translated this philosophy into the school setting by maintaining that, at the heart of the teaching process, the most decisive relationship is that of teacher and pupil. The teacher must establish the trust of students and be empathetic to them. Buber expected a great deal from teachers and saw them as more than simply facilitating the transfer of knowledge. In your own life, observe when you are in an I-Thou or I-It relationship; for instance, when you are buying a train ticket or at the checkout at a supermarket. Some stores are now training their staff to establish an I-Thou relationship with customers. Buber's influence on education can be seen in the work of current educational philosophers, such as Nel Noddings.

Nel Noddings (1929–), Professor of Education at Stanford University, challenges the belief that a general education based on the liberal arts is the best education for all. She is aware that 'criticising liberal education within academe is like criticising motherhood in a maternity ward'. She asserts that the current focus in schools – a narrow curriculum based largely on verbal and mathematical achievement – cripples many young people whose talents and abilities lie elsewhere. She believes that we need a radical change in both curriculum and teaching to reach all children, not just the few who fit our conception of the academically able. For her, the traditional organisation of schooling is intellectually and morally inadequate for contemporary society. She argues that the curriculum should be based on our growing understanding of multiple intelligences and the great variety and variability of children. Such a basis would support a drive for the human dimension to be put back into schools, which she sees as having become dehumanised. As a fundamental human need is to be cared for and to care, the general focus of the teacher should be to promote the concept of care, which would enable them to address the unique talents, abilities and interests of their children.

Noddings claims that the aim of education should be re-established as a moral one – of nurturing the growth of competent, caring, loving and loveable people. Such a moral purpose encourages the development of positive character traits, thereby supporting the advancement of schools that are moral in purpose, policy and methods. A negative outcome of the current education system is that a high proportion of pupils feel uncared for by schools. This is because teachers too often seem unable, perhaps through a perceived lack of time, to make connections with their students that sustain, in the student, a sense that adults care for them. In order to change this perception, those who have power over school systems need to give equal weight to academic and creative progress, and the development of relationships and character. This would allow teachers to legitimately give more time to the cultivation of I-Thou relationships. Noddings argues that, if pupils feel cared for through the modelling of this quality by teachers, they in turn learn the capacity to be more caring. She maintains that the key skill of the teacher is to care for the pupil. This can be demonstrated by listening to pupils' needs and interests, and then responding differentially, thereby helping them to develop the capacity to care for themselves, others, the environment, objects and ideas. Times to practice (e.g. community service) provide opportunities to gain skills in care-giving and to develop positive attitudes towards caring.

Why does Noddings reject liberal education as educationally inadequate? The history of liberal education is rooted in the classical education of gentlemen. It was used as a device to perpetuate a class structure, by only giving certain sections of the community access to it. In more recent years, a liberal education has become inappropriate for preparing students for life. It is often not seen as relevant to them. It propagates a myth that the same education is appropriate for all students and does not take account of the different capacities of individuals. Currently, schools around the world are urged by their governments to focus on the logical and mathematical capacities of students, often discriminating against those who possess other capacities, such as linguistic, musical, spatial, bodily/kinesthetic, interpersonal and intrapersonal skills.

The focus on logical-mathematical aspects, with its emphasis on rationality and abstract reasoning, neglects important features associated with feelings, concrete thinking, practical activity and moral action. What kind of education would we develop if we wanted our children to be kind, moderate and nurturing? Noddings argues that students need to develop the capacity to care for self, intimate others, distant others, the living environment, the world of objects and ideas. Teachers need to focus on the interests and capacities of pupils, engaging them in moral discourse. She argues that adults should talk to the children in their care about honesty, compassion, open-mindedness, non-violence, consideration, moderation and a host of other qualities that most of us admire.

So what should we conclude? This chapter has implied that Frankl, Aristotle, Montessori, Buber and Noddings represent a rich philosophical tradition, one based on the notion that young people should be helped to become the best people that they can possibly be. I suggest that the philosophy of valuing, which underpins values-based education, encapsulates and builds on the essence of this humane tradition. In the next chapter, we will consider where Frankl's 'search for meaning' begins.

Some reflection points to ponder from this chapter:

- Has there been a book that has profoundly affected you, as Frankl's affected me? If so, how has it consciously affected your thoughts and behaviour?

- Whose influence guides your behaviour as a parent or teacher, or in another aspect of your working life?

- What will you now consider doing differently because you have read this chapter?

Chapter 5

Children see, children do

I first met Cyril Dalais at the UNICEF headquarters in New York in the mid-1990s. Linda Heppenstall (values leader) and I, from West Kidlington School, were invited to be part of a working group of around thirty educators from around the world to establish a values programme that could be used globally. Cyril is a highly articulate and entertaining Mauritian, who brilliantly set the scene for a rationale of values education. I recall him asking: 'What is the root cause of so many problems in the world?' I remember us fumbling for answers and then he surprised us with a request. He said, 'Please imagine that you are holding a two-month-old child in your arms. If you are comfortable with demonstrating, then please show how you would hold the child.' (You might like to try this too!)

There were a number of reactions to this request: one man held his imagined child at arm's length and was greeted with laughter; others were tentative and unsure, but most held their pretend children. Cyril then asked two of us to carry our imaginary children to him and the rest of us put ours safely down. The chosen two stood on either side of Cyril and he asked us to notice how the children were being held. One was in a traditional cradle position; the other more upright with the child's head being supported so that the adult could look into the child's eyes or bring its head close to their body.

Cyril paused and then said: 'This is the most important action that a person does with a child. People hold young children in one of these two basic ways so that they can have eye-call with the child, and the child then feels safe and loved. The reason there are so many problems in the world is because an increasing number of children do not feel loved and are unable to develop a secure attachment with adults.' There was silence in the room as we took in the enormity of what Cyril was suggesting. Was his assertion correct? If you work in a school or meet a lot of children, then just consider for a moment the children who find good behaviour a challenge. Could it be the case that they lack secure attachment to an adult and intuitively feel a lack of being unconditionally loved?

I recall, as a head teacher, with my colleagues from West Kidlington, being asked by the local authority to support an inner city school in Oxford which was in difficulty. We were pleased to support the school and its community. I distinctly remember a winter's morning when I was meeting and greeting children as they arrived at the school. One child, six-year-old Alice, came up to me in floods of tears. I crouched down to her height and enquired, 'What's wrong Alice?' She could hardly get her words out as she said, 'Last night my Mum and Dad went up the pub and my brother was in left in charge. He brought in his mates and they put on a DVD. It was horrible! The adults were doing horrible things. I was frightened.' She couldn't go on and hyperventilated in a terribly distressed state. I called for support and we comforted Alice. Through social services, investigations revealed that what Alice had been subjected to was a violent pornographic movie which, in my opinion, no one should view, let alone a six-year-old child. These types of life experience can have a profound impact on a child. It is as though the experience forms a shell around them. My understanding is that we are born with tremendous potential and possess so many innate qualities. However, if these qualities are not nurtured, because of limiting or damaging life experiences, then there is a tendency to develop a negative self-image.

Such damaging experiences happen across the social spectrum, as was demonstrated whilst I was visiting a school in an advantaged area of Surrey. I was conducting an audit in a school that had applied for the International Values Education Trust (IVET) Quality Mark, when a mature-looking girl in a very smart school uniform with lots of badges approached me in the playground and enquired, 'May I have a word? Are you the visitor who has come to look at our values?' I smiled and replied that I was in the school to see how pupils were learning about values. She continued, 'My Daddy works in the city; he leaves early in the morning and returns home late at night. My Mummy goes to coffee mornings, I hardly see her. Our au pair looks after me. She takes me to ballet lessons, horse riding and swimming. Oh, and I have the latest iPad! The problem, you know, is that I feel so very unhappy at home. It'll soon be Christmas, and all I want for Christmas is for my parents to show they love and value me by being with me sometimes.' She didn't allow herself to cry, but turned away briskly and joined a group of Year 6 children who were chatting together.

Children who feel unloved or have suffered some form of abuse think of themselves as unlovable and many begin to believe that if they can't be loved for being good then they will be noticed by adopting challenging behaviours. This is exacerbated when the child is going through adolescence. Teachers of Year 9 pupils will recognise how children who have built up a series of negative life experiences from early childhood will be extremely difficult to motivate in the classroom. This is because we all have a basic human need to be recognised for who we are; secure, loving attachments enable us to develop a positive self-image. What does the values-based adult do to help such children? I believe that caring adults can metaphorically cut through all the layers of negative experiences that the child has suffered and connect with the child's essence, to qualities that may be lying dormant.

I watched a teacher in a Year 5 classroom ably demonstrate this. He had seen a boy from his class behaving badly at morning break. As the boy came into the classroom, the teacher quietly asked him over to his desk. He made eye contact and said, 'John, I know that we get on well together and I like you, but I saw you pushing another boy. Were you living up to our agreed values?' There was a pause as the boy looked away, obviously reflecting on his behaviour and the response he should give. After a few moments of deliberation, he looked back at the teacher and agreed that he was not living the school's values and that he should apologise and make amends to the other boy. What was so amazing about this simple interaction was that the teacher was firm, calm and clear about his expectations of the pupil's behaviour. However, what made this values-based teaching was the way that the teacher addressed the *behaviour* of the child and did not challenge his *person*, thereby skilfully maintaining the integrity of their relationship. I have already described (in Chapter 1) this subtle distinction, between the person and their behaviour, in relation to parents and their children.

Thea, a teacher I observed at Modbury Public School (Adelaide), uses a moral arbiter in the classroom to help children to think about their behaviour. This is Bob, the class skeleton, who acts as Thea's assistant. (I wonder if he was a former head teacher!) Picture the scene: two children have been misbehaving, so Thea says to them, 'Hey, what do you think Bob thinks of your behaviour? What would he tell you to do?' The children then describe what they think Bob would say, which is of course how they should be behaving. The simple device of having a Bob in the classroom means that the focus is taken away from what the teacher may think, or what the pupils perceive the teacher is thinking, to the children coming up with solutions by using their own moral compass based on their values. Through this simple ruse, the children learn greater self-awareness and to regulate their behaviour appropriately. Of course, Bob does not have to be a skeleton, which some of you may find ghoulish. I have seen a range of creatures and characters, such as bears, used in primary classrooms to similar effect. I am waiting to hear what could be the equivalent in business – any ideas?

In these examples, the teacher is conscious of being a values role model for the children, and of helping them to think and act from the base of an agreed set of values. I know from my own experience that being a role model is difficult to maintain. However, it is one of the key aspects of a values-based school and is based on the premise that what children see, children copy. Adults need to show children the kind of people that the world needs them to become. Whilst working in Australia, a teacher in Darwin suggested that I use a video in my presentations called, *Children See, Children Do.* If you have access to the Internet, then I invite you to watch it on YouTube. This powerful, distressing video portrays adults behaving badly in day-to-day situations. Children are seen copying adults who are smoking, shouting at someone from a different race, being abusive to another car driver and throwing litter in the street. One upsetting scene shows a father physically threatening his wife whilst his son joins in with blows to his mother. The point, dramatically made, is that children watch and then copy the behaviour of adults for good or ill. I showed this film to an audience of head teachers in the north of England and one came up to me at the end of the presentation to say that the police had recently visited her school because a pupil's father had been arrested for beating up his wife at home and had been assisted by the eight-year-old son!

Every experience we have in life impacts on us and leaves its impression on our psyche. A photo I love is of Sophie, who is shown at eighteen months in a strawberry field. She is holding a strawberry and gazing up with an amazing look of love to someone we can't see. I can't resist showing you the photo, so here it is:

Sophie is looking up at her mother, Madeline. You can see that Sophie is enjoying the experience and that her secure attachment with her mother is being positively reinforced. Research from neuroscience suggests that, as an adult, Sophie is unlikely to remember this event but, like all her experiences up until about the age of about three, it will form part of her implicit memory (unremembered as part of her personal narrative). It could also be called her somatic memory (having an effect on her body rather than her mind). Beyond three, Sophie will have the ability to recall experiences, which are then stored in her explicit memory, forming part of her personal narrative. She will see the world through her experiences as a child and make decisions about life based on them. A child who has challenging experiences of life, however, will see life through a negative lens. Neurobiology suggests that our early experiences affect the way that we are likely to parent our own children, which has enormous implications on the need for each one of us to work on our sense of self, thus ensuring that we don't transfer any limiting experiences from our own childhood to our children. In summary, this means that if we haven't formed secure attachments in childhood, then there is now an urgency to develop a secure attachment to ourselves. I believe that values-based education helps us to make new, positive decisions about how we see life.

I hope this chapter is prompting you to recall how you were parented and to consider the implications for how you now relate to others, both in your personal and your professional life.

Many aspects of our relationships are outside of our conscious awareness but, by pausing and considering how we relate to others in the home, school, business or community, we can take the opportunity to enhance them.

I believe it is important for each of us to cut through the layers of our own limiting experiences with a laser of healing, loving energy. Connect with that aspect of you that is still the little child. Give them your love; remind them that they are loved by you now. The good news is that, in a sense, *it is never too late to have a happy childhood*, because we can all begin to repair ourselves through the support of a values-based life ethic. There is no doubt that we are more able to love others if we feel loved by ourselves. Conversely, the popular media usually places an emphasis on trying to find happiness by loving others first.

Do you ever remember a teacher telling you that you couldn't sing? Or perhaps you were told that you couldn't draw, perform some aspect of physical activity or that you were poor at mathematics or English? When giving presentations, I am amazed to find people who remember being put down by a teacher when they were young for not being able to do something. I remember my daughter, Maddy, coming home one day from school, obviously very unhappy. I asked, 'What happened at school today?' She replied that she'd had an audition because she wanted to play the trumpet. The peripatetic music teacher had invited her and her best friend, Jo, to see if they were suited for the instrument. Maddy recalled that they were both asked to go to the music room. When they arrived, the teacher asked them both to pout their lips, and then he looked at Jo and said that she could learn the trumpet. He then took a long look at Maddy's lips and announced, 'Sorry, you have the wrong shaped lips to be a good trumpet player.'

Maddy said that she had rushed out of the room and made a beeline for the toilets, where she had burst into tears. A few minutes later, Jo found her and tried to comfort her. As her Dad, I felt outraged that she should have had such a humiliating experience. Maddy then took a sustained look at my lips and said, 'Daddy, you have the wrong shaped lips too!' We burst out laughing and a hug followed, which seemed to go a long way to putting the earlier event at school into perspective.

As you can see from Maddy's experience, teachers and other significant adults can have a considerable influence on a pupil's life and sense of self. What we do as children is to make agreements with adults in whom we believe. We make an assumption that what they say is true and it becomes an important part of how we see ourselves. My own personal experience poignantly illustrates this, as the following story illustrates.

I can still picture being a seven-year-old in Mr Smith's class at Lethbridge School, in Swindon. It was a big class – some fifty-four children (part of the post-war baby boom). My desk was at the side of the classroom, near to a window, through which I would often gaze and daydream. I particularly recall one occasion at the beginning of the autumn term when Mr Smith asked us to write about our summer holiday. The lesson routine was to write, draw an illustrative picture and then take it to the teacher's desk to be marked.

I had just returned from a holiday at Highcliff, near Bournemouth, where I had stayed in a caravan with my parents and brother, Maurice, so I had plenty to write about. I'd had a great time playing in the sea and building sandcastles. I could visualise the happy scene clearly in my mind. Industriously, I wrote the required half page with a picture of my brother and me playing in the water, which I drew in the plain paper space at the top. I glowed with the memories of my holiday and felt happy as I took my work to join the queue of children waiting in front of Mr Smith's desk. There were a number of children waiting – in those days, we would often play the queue game, which meant nearly getting to the front and then going to the back again! However, I wanted Mr

Smith to see my work because I thought he would be pleased with the way that I had written it.

Eventually, after a number of slow-moving minutes, I reached the Dickensian figure of Mr Smith (nicknamed Slipper Smith), whom I clearly remember with his half-rimmed glasses, over which he peered at us children. He took my work in his bony hands. There followed a long expectant pause: he kept looking at my work, staring at me and shaking his head disapprovingly and audibly tutting. With each of his gestures, my heart sank further, as this process seemed interminable. Then, in a somewhat snarling, sarcastic voice, and through clenched teeth, he pronounced loudly enough for the whole class to hear, 'Neil! Do you know, you can't write? You are just like your brother, Maurice, who used to be in my class. He couldn't write either! No capital letters, no full stops, awful spelling – this is dreadful. You just can't write and probably will never be any good as a writer. Do you know, you are a very stupid, pathetic, ignorant little boy.' He clipped me round the back of my head and raged, 'Go back to your desk and do it again and stop wasting my time, you imbecile.'

I returned to my desk, humiliated, dejected, tears flooding down my face, believing that I was a poor writer and a stupid person. The eyes of the other children seemed to burn into my head. I felt very hurt, put down and believed in my inadequacy, and these powerful feelings took root in my emerging sense of self. You see, that day, I had made an agreement with Mr Smith that I couldn't write – because little people agree with the views of big people – and that contract went through all my school days and into adulthood. I was left with a permanent sense of inadequacy and a nervous lack of self-respect when trying to write.

Years passed: I was in my head teacher's room at West Kidlington School, when John Heppenstall, one of the school's exceptionally talented senior teachers, came in and enthusiastically announced, 'Neil, I have so much respect for you. I think the *Dolphin News* [the parents' newsletter] you wrote this week is fantastic and so brilliantly crafted.' I heard myself replying, 'Come off it John, you're exaggerating. I'm not a very good writer – just do my best.' Exasperatedly, John said, 'Neil, it's really great. Who says you can't write?' I looked at John sheepishly and replied, 'Don't you know that Mr Smith said that I couldn't write!' John look bemused and said, 'Who the heck is Mr Smith?' So I explained to him about the legacy of my childhood experience. We then went on to discuss the effect teachers can have on children, both positive and negative. This event formed the basis of a discussion with teachers at the school about how we need to be aware of how a lack of respect for children can impact on their lives.

My question to all parents and teachers is: What agreements will children make with you? Will you nurture positive or negative messages? What Mr Smith did was criticise me ('You're stupid!') rather than constructively helping to improve my writing. I *implore* you to remember to build affirmative relationships with all children and inspire them to have confidence in themselves. In my view, a key task of a parent or teacher is to help the child to develop self-respect.

A teacher who had this crucial skill was Peter Long, the head teacher at South Stoke Village School (in Oxfordshire), a small school with two teachers. Peter taught the twenty-eight children in the class of seven- to eleven-year-olds. I had the privilege of working with him when I was on final teaching practice, during my training to be a teacher at Culham College of Education. Peter was all that Mr Smith wasn't – he was able to make a meaningful connection with every child in the school. He became my role model as I observed how he behaved as a teacher and a human being. I watched as Peter displayed his rich range of personal qualities. I recall, on one occasion, Peter talking with Justin, who reminded me of me when I was in Mr Smith's class. Justin was struggling to express himself in his story writing and Peter wanted to help him to master the basics, whilst not dampening his creativity. Peter suggested that Justin make a recording of his story on a tape recorder (yes, it was tape recorders in those days), which he did. Peter listened to the story and it created a vivid description of the countryside around South Stoke. Peter asked Justin if it could be played to the class. Justin agreed and what I witnessed was inspiring: after the tape finished, the children spontaneously clapped, and Justin glowed. I noticed that, after that lesson, Justin's work steadily improved, as he now realised that he was a writer and had lots of creative ideas. Peter's skills included the ability to listen deeply and attentively to children, maintain a positive manner and set appropriate boundaries. He believed that children deserve the very best from teachers and that being a positive role model is the most important characteristic of a good teacher.

A few years ago I was accompanying Professor Terry Lovat as part of our active support for the national values initiative in Australia. He took me to see Tracey Dennis's class at Wallsend South Public School (New South Wales). Tracey is an early years teacher and was then the teacher of a Young Starters class. Terry and I joined her class, on the carpet in a circle with the children. We watched Tracey weave her magic, giving each child every opportunity to develop a positive self-image, as they were sensitively encouraged to join in an action song. We observed how she acted as a superb role model for her class. I asked Tracey about what she thought had been the effects of values-based education at the school. She said:

> Since its inception, values-based education has changed the way teachers, parents and students think and feel in our school. The wider community often comments on its great spirit and the key to this is VbE. Through the implicit atmosphere of care and nurture and the explicit teaching of values in our school, we are now seeing evidence of students not only talking values but practising them. VbE affects everything, be it the signage, the assemblies, behaviour management, classroom teaching and many other features of the school. Importantly, it impacts positively on academic achievement as well. Children, teachers and parents work as one around VbE, creating a common language within the school and between the school and the home. We love our values school!

Whilst at the school, we also visited Renae Durbin's Year 5 class. She was sitting at her desk and the contrast with my own experience as a child with Mr Smith could not have been more stark. I watched as she talked with a pupil about her written work. I asked her to look up and I took her photo. Here it is:

What is it about this photo that makes you think that Renae is a values-based teacher? Some people have said that the clue is in the child who seems very comfortable with Renae, who is appropriately touching her with her arm around the child's shoulder. You will have noticed that the child is at ease and the engaging smile on each of their faces. In a values workshop for educational leaders I was conducting in the United Arab Emirates, a woman enthusiastically interjected, 'It's in her eyes!' Yes, she has smiling eyes! A school inspector once asked me if I could provide a list of competencies that good teachers should possess. I remember pausing and replying that there is really only one – the eyes. Has the teacher got smiling eyes? I am grateful to Professor Bart McGettrick for first bringing the concept of smiling eyes to my attention. If you are near someone at the moment, have a look at their eyes and see whether they are smiling. Are yours smiling? If you are carrying the cares of the world on your shoulders then it will show in your eyes. When we work with children, we must ensure that we engage with them from a place of positivity and an attitude of can-do.

I recall receiving an e-mail from a teacher in Brisbane, who asked me if I remembered asking an audience to look at the person next to them and to see if their eyes were smiling. He wanted me to know that he had just married the person whose eyes he had looked into! Getting back to Renae, what I think she demonstrates is *unconditional positive regard* for the child. This term, first coined by the influencial psychologist Carl Rogers, is key to ensuring that we act as a values-based adult – one who is genuine, open and honest in their communication, who really sees the other person, accepts them and has empathy, so that they genuinely feel listened to and understood. Renae and her pupil brilliantly demonstrate one of the main research outcomes of a values-based school, *relational trust*.

This chapter has been about children seeing and children doing, meaning that values-based education begins with adults who become conscious about their own behaviour and how this influences the development of children. This point has to be acknowledged and understood before we can ask the question of the next chapter: So what's a value?

Some reflection points to ponder from this chapter:

- Please review your own childhood and the attachments you made with adults. Think about the positive ones and any that were limiting. Health warning: if this is potentially a distressing experience, then please seek the help of someone who can counsel and support you.

- Give time to directing your own loving energy to any situation that you found challenging as a child. Transform any negative thoughts you may have by forgiving yourself and anyone else who may have upset you. You might have to allocate time on successive days to this activity to support the healing process.

- If you have children of your own, consider how you are helping them to develop a secure attachment to you. How are you ensuring that you are giving them your love and sufficient time?

- How do you show unconditional positive regard to others?

Chapter 6

So what's a value?

I ended the previous chapter with the title of this chapter. Please give a few moments to considering this question about values.

Can you think of a definition that you could give to a child?

From experience, whenever I ask this question, I find that people find it quite difficult to give a succinct answer; it is much easier to be asked to name some values, such as cooperation, honesty or compassion. Academics have written extensively about values, but I think we need to have a working definition that can form the basis of our understanding about values. I have found that children can remember the following definition:

A value is a principle that guides our thinking and behaviour.

Of course, there is a need to explore what we mean by the words in this sentence, such as *principle*. Words like source, origin, standard, belief, attitude and code come to mind. Some people prefer a slightly expanded definition, such as: 'Values are the principles, fundamental convictions and standards that act as the general guides to our behaviour and thinking.' Whatever daily decisions or actions we take in life, I believe that it is our values that determine their quality.

Values help to determine the formation of our character. When we actively engage with our innate values, we start to understand their implications for making choices about our attitudes and responses. Values are transmitted through the quality of our relationships. Having relationships that are attuned to others is crucial and this is gained by having sufficient self-knowledge to enable us to empathise with others. Having attuned relationships is also a key to good parenting. An important predictor for being a well-adjusted child is the degree of self-knowledge or self-awareness of the adult caregiver. This skill is linked to the adult's ability to model values. The less self-aware adult is less likely to give children a sense of positive values. I recall chatting to Bob, the site manager of Lyneham Primary School (in Wiltshire), who told me that he had been a soldier in Bosnia and was assigned to guard an orphanage. The effect of getting to know these children was so profound that, on his return to civilian work, he wanted a job that helped and supported children, hence his current role at Lyneham.

The values that we hold in our hearts are expressed in our behaviour and can be described as our *virtues* (qualities such as being wise, courageous or peaceful) – in my view, an underused term nowadays. Our virtues can be observed in the action of our lives and can be described as our *living values*. Aristotle, my Greek philosopher hero, put it this way: 'By imitating virtue, we become virtuous.' He suggested that the virtues start with *politeness*, which is the beginning of respect and gratitude – where morality begins. We can then develop other dispositions such as *prudence*, which allows us to think about what is good for us. 'Prudence', he said, 'governs other virtues, such as temperance, courage and justice.' I mentioned earlier that in 2006 I took an active speaking role in an education conference in Edinburgh. The principal speaker was the inspirational Dalai Lama, who on the subject of virtue referred to what he had written about it in his book *Ancient Wisdom, Modern World* (1999):

> In order for our actions to become spontaneously ethical, it requires us to put the pursuit of virtue at the *heart* of our daily lives. We gain experience of virtue through constant practice so that it becomes spontaneous … we need to transform our habits and dispositions.

If, because of the changing nature of society, some of the traditional routes of values development no longer exist, what can be done to promote an understanding about values? I have noted that for children to access mathematics they need a mathematical language, to access science they need a scientific language and so on. Therefore, I think that to access ethics (a code of morality – the inner impulses, judgements and duties of people) children need to be introduced to an ethical vocabulary. Values words such as honesty, respect and trust create such an ethical vocabulary, which can then act as a guide to how they live their lives. Indeed, I believe that it gives children an ethical intelligence; that is, the ability to be self-aware in order to consider their thoughts and actions, and the actions of others. This can be achieved through values-based education, which evolves when an educational setting, such as a school, underpins everything it does from the perspective of universal, positive human values. This encourages reflective and aspirational attributes and attitudes, which can be nurtured to help young people discover the very best of themselves, which then enables them to act as responsible, humane citizens. Such future citizens are more likely to contribute to a national democratic culture, which is strengthened by the value of trust and supported by values such as respect, tolerance, equity, cooperation, openness, justice and transparency.

I use the term *positive* because I distinguish between two types of values: positive and potentially limiting. Examples of positive values include responsibility, care and respect. Greed and selfishness are limiting values – they limit our potential to be humane. The word *universal* reminds us that positive values are shared universally throughout the world. They are *human values* and are supported by the majority of people, no matter what religion they may espouse or if they are non-religious. It has been heart warming to observe that the majority of people appreciate what I am saying and understand why there is a need to highlight these attributes with young people.

I have had only one parent who has openly disagreed with me. I was giving a talk in London to a group of parents and a father said that he didn't agree with the school's values work. I asked him why. He replied that he was a second-hand car salesman and therefore he didn't want his son to be honest because he couldn't be! Everyone laughed and I think (hope) he was joking. I also remember a parent talking with me at West Kidlington School, who said that she had thought that values education was nonsense until one day at home when she was busy getting the evening meal ready for the family and feeling a bit moody.

Her daughter, Cindy, came into the kitchen and said, 'Mum, you're not showing much patience!' She then knew that there must be something in this values stuff. An amusing story, but it does show how children who are learning about values can begin to raise awareness of them at home.

Not only parents see the value of values. You will be interested to know that leaders and adherents of all the great religions, including Buddhism, Christianity, Hinduism and Islam, support the development of values-based education, as do non-religious groups such as humanists. I think that beliefs can divide people, whereas values unite them; we can all work to develop universal, positive human values.

For instance, the values-based school takes time to think about how to develop and express values. It aims to inspire pupils, as a form of character education, to live the values in their lives: to be the best people they can possibly be. This is a crucial point, as institutions can espouse values (e.g. on their websites) but not really live them. I was talking recently to some senior students at a secondary school in the UK and was asking them if the school's values were having an impact on the school and the lives of the people in it. I was amazed when a boy said that he was concerned that although members of staff wanted the students to follow a code of values, not all staff were living the values. I asked for an example and he mentioned a science teacher, a strict disciplinarian who was always telling students to adhere to the school's values. However, the teacher had been observed riding his motorbike and 'jumping' the local traffic lights when they were red. The values-based school should inspire both adults and pupils to live the values in their lives, so it is important that all adults are consistent in modelling them.

To ensure consistency, it is vital that, before committing to developing values-based education, the school is clear about why it wants to move to a values-based approach. In conversation with the leadership of a school, I would ask the following questions: Have you seen a values-based school, read about one or considered the research evidence for developing as one? Will the initiative have the active support of the head or principal and the school's senior leadership team?

I have had the privilege of working with many leaders, both in education and in other sectors of society. I am convinced that an institution will find it impossible to be values-based if the leader's values are not centred on universal, positive human values. Richard Barrett, founder of the Barrett Values Centre, whose company has researched the culture of schools, large corporations and countries, says:

> The culture that you find in a school is a reflection of the values of the head or principal. If you want to change the culture of a school, then the head or principal must either change his or her values, or you must change the head or principal. Organisational transformation begins with the personal transformation of the leaders. Who you are and what you stand for as a leader has a significant impact on the culture of the group you are responsible for.

If the leader is fully committed to the values dynamic, then practical considerations need to be addressed, such as: Who will take the lead on values development? Will it be a mixture of people from the school and community? Are you prepared to invest the necessary time, energy and resources? Have you considered the timescale for implementation, success criteria and how you will monitor and evaluate the process of implementation? Have you realised that values-based education is about cultural transformation, and sharply challenges personal assumptions and mindsets about the nature of education, schooling and life in general? It is important to audit how things are at present; for example, the school's climate for teaching and learning, relationships, level of synergy or cooperation in the staff and the educational philosophy of the school. Ask: How does our school currently impart values to pupils? What are these values and on what basis have they been chosen? Are they taught implicitly or explicitly? How will you address the potential toxic one or two per cent of your community who will not adhere to the values? What do you hope will be the benefits of adopting the values-based approach? Such questions help in understanding that values-based education is a unique transformative whole-school process for sustainable school improvement. It is rooted in an educational philosophy, one that I have termed the *philosophy of valuing*, which is a new paradigm for conscious cultural change, encouraging people to develop reflective practices, self-control and self-responsibility for behaviour and actions. The philosophy extends far beyond the school into every aspect of society.

My overarching vision is for the development of a values-based global society, as I believe that, for humanity to flourish in the twenty-first century, nations urgently need a conscious cultural transformation based on universal, positive human values. Failure to embrace such a paradigm shift will inevitably increase what Richard Barrett refers to as the level of 'cultural entropy' (Barrett, 2010), which can be explained as the amount of energy in us that is consumed in unproductive work: the measure of the conflict, friction and frustration that exists within a group, even a nation. For a society to avoid the destructive destabilisation that comes from its people perceiving that national values are unjust, leaders are required who embrace and model positive values. Such transformational leaders implicitly embrace the Greek concept of *physis* (the creative, life-sustaining force of nature). They are aware that a just and sustainable society is based on the mutual trust of its leaders and citizens. They influence all institutions of state to be values-based and encourage the development of successful and sustainable values-driven communities and organisations. Articles of government at national and local level safeguard the rights of citizens and encourage an ethic of responsibility for the good of all. Such leadership demands much more than rhetoric, as leaders are expected to be good examples of positive values by living them in their personal and professional lives. Consistency, in terms of agreed behaviours that reflect positive values, creates trust between leaders and the general public.

Back to the school. If a school decides that it wants to implement the philosophy of valuing, along with its practices, then I would suggest that it invests in the following process that answers the question: How do you introduce values? The whole school community (staff, pupils, parents and community representatives) is involved in understanding, identifying and shaping the values education policy. A meeting or forum is set up to facilitate this process. The forum will propose that the school adopts universal, positive human values – such as respect, honesty and cooperation – to underpin everything it does (i.e. all administrative and organisational practices and the curriculum). These values are chosen through a careful process that involves thinking about what qualities (values) the school should encourage its pupils to develop.

I recently facilitated a forum at Downley Primary School (in High Wycombe). Sue Webb, the head teacher, had previously invited me to work with the whole of her staff at a values in-service training day. Following this, she had surveyed her teaching and support staff to gauge their backing for introducing values-based education. She found that there was overwhelming support. The following was a typical view: 'Sue, I wanted to give you my feedback on today, *wow*, what an inspiration, sign me up!'

Following the staff training day, parents and members of the community were invited to take part in the values forum. The school took care that this would be an enjoyable occasion with refreshments and comfortable seats around tables with A3 sheets of paper, pens and dictionaries. About a hundred people were warmly greeted and there was a very positive relational atmosphere in the room as I set the scene for the evening. In my general introduction to values-based education, I asked the audience to reflect on what they thought were the values that they currently saw as underpinning society. Greed, selfishness and consumerism were mentioned. I then asked what three values influenced their personal behaviour. Quite a different list emerged: care, responsibility and love.

When I judged that everyone in the values forum had a clear understanding about the importance of values in general, I then asked them to answer the following question: If you could encourage children to live one value, what would it be? After a pause, I then invited them to argue the case for their value with the other people on their table and challenge why others thought that their value was more important. I was delighted because everyone joined in the spirit of the evening, arguing forcefully for their favourite value. Meanings of the values were explored and folk justified why their value was the most valuable. After a while, I asked everyone to pause and invited each table to find consensus on two values that they could all agree were the most important. This process took a few more minutes; then I invited each table to let the forum know their chosen values. These were recorded on a whiteboard by one of the teachers. If more than one table repeated a value, then it was given a tick on the list. We soon had a list of values, with *respect* receiving the most ticks. I then invited everyone to think whether any really important value had been omitted. Someone suggested that *compassion* should be added and after more discussion the addition was agreed.

The list of values that had been agreed at the forum was then circulated the next day to all parents for consultation and endorsement, so that everyone in the community was aware of the values that had been agreed and had the opportunity to give their opinion. Downley School has carefully monitored its values programme to assess its impact on pupil behaviour. Parents and community members continue to be engaged in the process through forum meetings.

I cannot stress enough how important it is to ensure that everyone has the chance to be involved in the process of identifying the values that the school is going to teach. If they are, then each person feels ownership of the values. Some schools tell me that they have a list of values, so I ask them to tell me about how they were chosen. Responses include: 'our governors' chose them' or 'our head teacher made up the list'. However, a typical forum produces a list which may look similar to this:

Peace	Quality
Respect	Hope
Love	Patience
Happiness	Caring
Freedom	Trust
Responsibility	Understanding
Honesty	Justice
Humility	Courage

Tolerance	Friendship
Compassion	Thoughtfulness
Cooperation	Unity

When a school's community has recommended which values should be taught, then the school – perhaps the values coordinator, the values action team or the senior leadership team – makes the final decision about which values comprise the final list. The governors or school board of the school then endorse this list as the school's values.

Helen Snowden, at Lethbridge School (in Swindon), inspired the display of her school's values on the wall of the school hall in the following creative way:

Seaford 6–12 School (a large middle and high school in the southern suburbs of Adelaide) undertook a notable variation of this process. I visited the school and met the principal, Mary Asikas, who wanted her 925 students and eighty staff to be fully engaged in creating a shared direction for the school. She set up a two-day workshop, facilitated by a team from Quality Learning Australia, in which the students and staff would consider the vision, values and behaviours they wanted for their school. The outcome was a school vision which stated:

Our students' well-being and growth are achieved through:

- A focus on positive relationships

- A rich and diverse curriculum

which meets the needs of all our students.

The values selected were learning, listening, respect, friendship, happiness and responsibility. The outcome of the workshop was transformative, with the staff realising the importance of modelling the school's values and giving students positive recognition. The students reported significant changes because of the positive change in school culture. For instance, before the values forum there was disrespectful behaviour and some fighting among students, but afterwards students were taking better care of each other. The school put the agreed values and associated behaviours on large quality notices around the school as a guide to life. For instance, the notice about the value of respect had a series of 'I' statements, such as, 'I am courteous', 'I am fair', 'I respect others' ideas, needs, opinions and beliefs' and 'I treat others equally'.

I recommend that all institutions, such as companies, businesses and public services (such as the police and hospitals), use a modification of the values selection process that suits their context in determining their values. My vision is that towns and cities will be inspired to be values-based. As I write, I am aware that Skövde (in Sweden) and Helmond (in the Netherlands) are keen to be among the first values-based cities in Europe. It is this process of values identification and clarification that creates the ethical vocabulary, or common language, which builds ethical intelligence.

Nevertheless, I find that the most challenging part of the process is to gain the agreement of adults to model the values that have been selected. It is important that individuals are given space and adequate time to consider what behaviours they are going to adopt or stop, so that they become role models for values. This process requires a spirit of open and honest communication in a supportive atmosphere. It may be helpful to have some ground rules for thinking about our behaviours. For instance, not to be personal or to take the discussion personally; to be open to our own process that may make us feel uncomfortable or defensive; to recognise that many of our behaviours are habitual and are outside of our conscious awareness; to conduct the occasion seriously but with appropriate humour. The more that the group of adults feel comfortable with each other, the easier this session will be. It is important that everyone feels heard and their opinion valued. I would recommend that the session is facilitated by someone who is well respected and perceived as not having ulterior motives (i.e. someone who isn't involved in determining the pay and conditions of service of employees).

Be prepared for the session to be controversial: after all, folk are invited to take a value such as respect and think about how they will model it. For instance, is it appropriate for staff to shout at pupils, use sarcasm or put-downs if the school promotes the value of respect? How would you answer members of staff who say that they get respect from students by shouting at them? Or who believe that students have to experience firm discipline in order to develop respect? Or that the students should always hold doors open for staff and not wait for adults to hold doors? Or that if we are teaching our students good manners, surely they must show respect to us first? Not all values have the potential to be controversial, but this session will expose differences based on the adults' previous experience, background and culture.

The leadership of the school will need to adjudicate, making it clear how the desired behaviours will reflect the school's intended culture, vision and statement of values. Once an agreement is reached, then I recommend that the behaviours are noted in job descriptions and become a part of performance management and advertisements for vacancies. This recommendation may seem a bit intrusive, but it is vital in order to achieve consistency of adult behaviour across the institution. If this is not achieved, then students will notice the lack of consistency and be less inclined to practise the values in their own lives.

I have found that this process creates harmony and makes working in the institution easier and more enjoyable, as a common culture emerges based on the adopted values. There is a sense of creativity and freedom as people take responsibility for their behaviour in a more conscious way. I am reminded of a short video that shows a goldfish in a bowl in a sitting room. It is watching the television through the bowl and can see salmon leaping up a river. The goldfish decides to escape and swim with the salmon. The video takes us on the journey of the goldfish, who avoids all sorts of calamities to finally reach the river with the salmon. This is a wonderful metaphor for the values-based school that empowers both adults and students to take control of their behaviour in order to live their values, and therefore lead happy and productive lives.

So far in our journey through this book, we have considered the underlying philosophy of values-based education. I hope that you have come to appreciate that it is a philosophy of being and living, which permeates policy and day-to-day practice. Its power is that it enables people to think through, develop and espouse a normative set of values that create an ethical vocabulary (a common language), which enables them to develop self-knowledge. Values-based education helps people to achieve a 'good life' by encouraging a shift away from self-focus to a community focus and towards 'actions of goodness'. My wife, Jane, having insights from her psychotherapeutic background, refers to values-based education as 'a lifeline for some children and a life enhancer for all'. In essence, it is a transformative tool which enables young people to sense and shape their future, giving meaning and purpose to their lives.

However, I have reached the conclusion that it is mainly the values that adults model which have the most profound effect, for good or ill, on influencing the values development of the young. No manual for values education can replace the influence of family, carers, teachers and significant others on the sustainable development of our society. The next ten chapters will answer the question: What does a values-based school or setting do that is different?

Some reflection points to ponder from this chapter:

- What is a value? How can you help others to understand?

- Which themes or points in this chapter have impacted on you? What actions will you take?

- You may decide to go through a process of identifying a set of values with those with whom you live.

Chapter 7

Focus on environment, atmosphere and routines

Having read the previous chapters, I wonder what you think a values-based school does that is different from other schools?

I would like to invite you to pause and reflect on this question. What clues have I been giving you? I hope there will be synergy between your thoughts and mine.

Pause ...

Before I answer the question, I want to describe what a values-based school has that is similar to all good schools.

Firstly, it has good leadership that has a clear vision and high expectations for the school, which will ensure that it is managed effectively. Secondly, it has a relevant curriculum that engages students as active learners. Thirdly, it has teachers who understand how children learn best, who have a deep understanding of pedagogy (the science of teaching) and aim for high standards.

What makes the values-based school different is that it also consciously and explicitly underpins everything it thinks about and does with universal, positive human values. I believe that schools in the twenty-first century require all these elements in order to create learning and teaching environments that are outstanding – that nurture every aspect of children so that they are truly educated as wise, knowledgeable, compassionate human beings. I believe this so passionately that, a few years ago, I wanted to make the evidence available to the UK government, perhaps somewhat naively thinking that there would be enthusiasm for creating the first explicitly values-based nation.

At this time, Bridget Knight, who as a senior education adviser responsible for inspiring the development of values-based education in Herefordshire, was present with me at 10 Downing Street in London. We had been invited to give a presentation about values-based education to one of Tony Blair's policy advisers. I recall him asking us, 'What does a values school do that is different from others?' The adviser listened attentively as we answered his question, pointing out what would be gained by our country if there were to be a focus on universal, positive human values. The session concluded with him recognising the potential of values to make a difference, but saying regretfully that, as the Blair government was coming to an end, it would be unlikely that values-based education would receive any formal or tacit backing. In hindsight, I am happy with this outcome, because values-based education could rightly be viewed suspiciously if it were perceived to be the tool of a particular political party, whether from the left or right, intent on a form of social control. However, I have continued to give my support to countries, education systems and school communities that can see the benefits of values-based education – the government of the United Arab Emirates is currently in this category.

Let us return to the vital question: What does a values-based school or setting do that is different? I think this question is best answered in the context of what I call the 10Fs (or focuses) of VbE, which I will describe in the following chapters. It is these ten dimensions that act as a checklist for implementing values-based education. They are worked on concurrently – not in list order – as the community moves towards being values-based. I am indebted to the many values-based education practitioners in numerous countries who have shared their ideas and whose good practices I have used in this book. I also strongly believe that research evidence should inform the development of good practice. With this in mind, I have drawn on the studies into the effectiveness of values education produced by Professor Terry Lovat and others at Newcastle University, New South Wales, and my own research at Oxford University.

Please continue to enjoy reading, even if you are not involved directly in education, as you will find it fascinating to apply the underlying principles in each chapter to your own context, whether it is a public or private sector organisation, company, business or your own family.

The 10Fs of VbE

1 **Focus on environment, atmosphere and routines**

   Aim to have a calm and purposeful atmosphere. Carefully ensure that the internal and external environment reflect positive values. Question aspects of organisation and routines that may inhibit the promotion of good practices.

2 **Focus on you**

   The values-based setting encourages the valuing and well-being of self and others.

3 **Focus on your relationships**

   It is OK to have a hierarchy of roles, but never a hierarchy of relationships.

4 **Focus on adopting reflective practices**

   Encourage the skill of reflection, which is the ability to access the internal world of thoughts and feelings, and to regulate them.

5 **Focus on an ethical vocabulary**

   Establish and consistently use a common and shared values language.

6 **Focus on being a role model for values**

Implicitly model values and explicitly foster the modelling of values.

7 **Focus on school assemblies**

Assemblies and other meetings are important for the conscious transmission of culture.

8 **Focus on the school's curriculum and its leadership**

Think of values as an integrated curriculum concept, rather than as a programme, an event or an addition to the curriculum. Develop values-based leadership.

9 **Focus on community**

A values-based setting is outward looking. It works with and in the community.

10 **Focus on values assessment**

Monitor the effects of values-based education and evaluate its effectiveness. Remember to celebrate your success.

In this and the next nine chapters, we will have a closer look at each of these 10Fs, starting with the environment, but please remember that in practice we focus on all aspects simultaneously.

Focus on environment, atmosphere and routines

Have you ever taken the time to look consciously at a school's main entrance, especially its doors? Such a question is not in a school inspector's manual, but I believe it gives significant clues about what sort of institution it is, in terms of its relationship with the community and what its priorities are. The first aspect of what I term *institutional values* (values that are evident in an organisation that are often outside of conscious awareness) is to notice whether, on arrival at the school, the indications are that you are welcome. In the UK, unlike countries such as Australia, Iceland and Sweden, many schools have been made into 'fortresses' because of health and safety concerns created by a few high profile atrocities against staff and children. Whilst I am appalled by these cases and think that all reasonable care should be taken to protect staff and students, I sometimes question whether many of the safety precautions act more as a greater deterrence to law-abiding citizens than they ever would to a criminal who would simply break a window to get in. In some countries, such as the United States, which has the highest proportion of private gun ownership in the world, social attitudes exacerbate the need for an extreme focus on safety, such as armed police patrolling high schools and metal detectors to identify students who are carrying weapons.

If you currently have a child of primary school age, may I suggest that when you visit their school take time to look at the main entrance to the building. What messages does it give you? Are there notices on the doors or walls? If so, what do they say? Here are some examples I have

seen: 'Welcome to our school', 'Please call at reception', 'Leave your prams outside', 'CCTV is used here', 'All visitors *must* report to reception'. My daughter Katherine, who is a social worker, sent me a photograph of a big poster that she noticed outside a primary school.

The school in question had obviously been having problems with uninvited people parking their cars in the school grounds. The solution did not account for the perception of very young children, who would see the picture on the notice but would not be able to read what was written beneath it: 'Parking for school staff only'. Put yourself in the place of a three-year-old non-reader coming to a playgroup. How would you feel if you saw this notice? You probably would feel sad or wonder why people at the school are cross.

So many signs that I see in institutions are displayed with little thought for the unintended impact they can have. Generally, they seem to be outside of the conscious awareness of most people. Hospitals and parks sometimes have very unfriendly notices. Keep a look out for them as you walk around towns. When deciding to develop values-based education audit your signs and notices to check that the wording reflects your values. For instance, a sign that says 'All visitors must report to the school office', can be changed to 'Please will all visitors report to the school office'. Both notices convey the same meaning, but with a different tone which create different feelings in us. The external environment should remind us about the school's values. A notice proclaiming that the school is values based, with perhaps a values mosaic, sculpture or other creative artwork, lets the community and visitors know about the values philosophy and practices that will be found there. Play equipment can be marked in a creative design with the school's values too. The arrangement and type of play equipment, the way that outside areas are designed and equipped, including seating, all indicate how children are valued in the school. Look out for concrete deserts, graffiti, ceiling panels that look like they will fall down and guttering precariously hanging from the roof – all features that I have seen when auditing schools around the world.

On entering a values-based school, you should be able to detect a calm and purposeful atmosphere – a reflection of the quality of internal stability and mutually agreed direction of staff. Such an atmosphere can be detected in schools such as Madley (in Herefordshire) which has a water feature, Greenfield (in Bedfordshire) which has calming music and St Charles Boremeo (in Melbourne) which has Sue Cahill, the well-being coordinator, with her infectious enthusiasm, twinkle in her eye and broad smile. Such schools give a great deal of thought and care to these features. This ensures that the internal and external school environment reflects the school's values, encourages their students to take responsibility to be active participants in their learning and thereby develop *agency* – a research outcome of values-based education.

Values-based institutions often have checklists that they use to audit the ambience of their environment. Questions might include: What do visitors tell you about your atmosphere? Is it generally calm or is it frenetic? How do leaders model being calm? Are they good listeners or do they talk at people? What tone of voice is encouraged in the school? Are good manners given a high profile? How are they expressed? How are visitors greeted at reception? Do you use an answerphone? Is it people friendly? (Whilst working in Tasmania, I was sent an amusing spoof school answerphone message by e-mail. The disembodied sounding voice said, 'Dial 1 to report your child's absence, 2 to be rude to a teacher, and 3 to assault the principal!')

Another action: take a look at school displays and ensure that they reflect agreed values. For instance, if the school has a display of staff photographs, check if it is arranged in a relational or hierarchical way. Photographs with the leader at the top and a cleaner at the bottom could imply that one person thinks that they are superior – a hierarchy of relationships. Seaford 6–12 High School (near Adelaide) has a display of staff photos in its entrance area arranged within a circle. Each person's role is labelled (hierarchy of roles) but the implied message is that everyone is an equal human being. Remember this catchy phrase which I have used a number of times in this book: a values-based institution does not have a hierarchy of relationships, only a hierarchy of roles. Avoid using *must* and *don't* in signs. I know (you may think similarly) what I am tempted to do if I read, 'Don't walk on the grass!' When we read a negative message, our brains turn it into a positive one, so *don't* becomes *do*.

In recent years, I have followed Jamie Oliver's lead by taking an interest in school meals. Whereas Jamie looks at the quality of the food, I am interested in the arrangements that are made (or not made) to make lunchtime a civilised, values-based process. Arrangements vary drastically from country to country and within countries. Tracey Smith, head teacher at Tower Hill Primary School (in Witney), made hers the most improved school in Oxfordshire (Standard Assessment League Tables) by addressing *all* aspects of the school's organisation, including lunchtime arrangements. In previous years, the pupils had lined up at a serving hatch in the school hall to collect their food on purpose-designed plastic trays. They were served their lunch by kitchen staff and then chose a place at one of the tables to sit to eat. On finishing their meals the children left the hall. There was little sense of a shared social experience. I have seen this method countless times throughout the world. It could be termed a functional arrangement, but sadly it is not relational and nor does it add quality to the eating experience.

In consultation with the staff, Tracey decided to introduce a form of 'family service' where children and adults would sit at large tables in groups of twelve. Children now take turns to serve each other and no one on a table leaves until everyone has finished. Louise Conroy, the values coordinator, told me that the arrangement has made a big difference to the children's social skills and the general tone of lunchtimes. Prime Minister David Cameron has visited the school, which is in his constituency, and praised its achievements. He said on Witney TV: 'This is a school that has really improved in terms of the results it is getting and through the support of the values which I have seen in the school myself.' Congratulations to Tower Hill School!

The quality of lunch arrangements at Tower Hill reminds me of many Swedish schools, where I have found the quality of food and lunch arrangements to be some of the best in the world. For instance, at Eriksdal (in Skövde), Camilla Wallin, the school's director, invited me to experience a typical Swedish lunch with the children. All pupils have a school meal and no charge is made to families as it is paid for through general taxation. The quality of the food is superb, as are the arrangements for enjoying the meal in a social setting. A week later, I was experiencing a school lunch in another country where the experience could be likened to mayhem, the noise level being quite unacceptable and the children rushing their food with the minimum of adults present. At the end of the meal, lunchtime staff were seen clearing the tables by wiping the leftover food onto the floor, only to be walked on by children leaving the hall! This school could learn from the example of Madley School (in Herefordshire) where each table has a copy of the 'Manners Menu' for all to see.

Let's think about other aspects of school organisation and routines. A question I often ask a school is whether they are in the twenty-first century or still promoting aspects of the nineteenth. St Ambrose College (in Hale, near Manchester) has a new building that is designed for twenty-first century learning. The head teacher, Michael Thompson, has resisted putting any form of promotional display in the main school entrance, maintaining that the values and aims of the school can be seen in the quality of behaviour and relationships of the students. Other schools may not be as conscious about why they continue certain routines.

There may be good reasons for maintaining established practices, but I encourage schools to examine the reasoning behind them and whether they are values based and promote the educational vision of the school. For instance, why are children lined up in playgrounds at the end of break times in primary schools? There may be good grounds to continue this practice, but many schools do not line children up, instead expecting them to walk sensibly into school. At others, a whistle will be blown, which is the signal for the children to stand still. The teacher on duty then holds up coloured cards, each colour indicating a year group of children who should walk into their classes. On one school visit, I recall timing how long it took lunchtime supervisors to line up children in the playground and to get them into classrooms. It was an astounding seventeen minutes! I watched as children were shouted at to be quiet, some were sent to the back of the line and others were threatened with being reported to the head teacher. During this process, the adults got increasingly upset and the children very unsettled. I wondered if there was an implicit collusion going on to delay the start of afternoon lessons.

The use of bells in schools is another issue to be questioned. In some secondary schools, ferocious-sounding bells ring to denote the end of a lesson. Students react to the bell and start to leave the room before being told by the teacher. They respond in ways similar to the experiment conducted by Pavlov, who found that dogs learn to salivate on hearing a bell because they knew that it indicated the arrival of food. Many secondary schools have stopped using bells, expecting instead that adults and students will take responsibility for time-keeping and establishing a routine to ensure that all clocks in the school reflect the time accurately. Another aspect to consider concerns the use of words that do not represent a relational values-based school; for instance, *targets* (a military term), *detention* and *rules*, rather than values and agreed charters.

I hope that you are not thinking that I am promoting a school system that represents a laissez-faire, do as you like, anything goes, free-for-all attitude. On the contrary, I believe that there should be consequences for inappropriate actions, but that these consequences are brought on ourselves because we have failed to live up to our values. Good parenting and good teaching sustains the child in a secure, caring relationship, but holds them accountable for their behaviour. A values-based school therefore puts an emphasis on young people taking responsibility for their actions.

I recall Eugene Symonds (fondly nicknamed Nudge during his rugby-playing days), the current head of West Kidlington School, recounting an incident at lunchtime when a child was sent to have a word with him because of poor behaviour in the playground. Nudge listened to the child and, before making comment, asked him to go and spend a few minutes looking at the values display in the school hall, to think about the values displayed there and what he had done in the playground. The child went away and shortly returned. Nudge asked him what he had been thinking about. The boy said that he had looked at the word *respect* and realised that he hadn't been showing respect either to the dinner staff or his classmates. The boy went on to say, without any prompting, that he should go and apologise, and that he would be careful not to repeat his bad behaviour in the future. This is a good example of how children can be helped to self-regulate their behaviour. There is no doubt that other more traditional forms of discipline may control children's behaviour, but there is scant evidence that they help them to act from a code of ethics rather than from the fear of punishment.

Values-based schools have high expectations about behaviour and give opportunities from an early age for children to take responsibility for their actions. I recall visiting Valgerður Knútsdóttir's wonderful pre-school for children between the ages of one and six in Iceland, and witnessing the carefully crafted routines that are established there to nurture the value of responsibility. One was to have a photograph of each of the children: on one side was the child's face and on the reverse was the back of the head. If a child is present in the classroom, then they turn the photo of their face facing outwards and if they leave the room, perhaps to visit the toilet, then they turn the photo so that the back of the head is showing. Such simple routines define a values-based school with an attention to detail, which can empower children to be responsible for their own behaviour and grow to be the best people that they can possibly become.

I hope this chapter has helped you to think about the environment in which you live and work. May I ask that, when you enter your place of work, you pause and imagine that you are seeing it for the first time. Ask yourself to what extent it represents positive human values and consider what actions, if any, you need to make. The next chapter puts the spotlight on you!

Some reflection points to ponder from this chapter:

- Would you describe your environment as values based? Audit your signage and daily routines and ask what values they reflect.

- How would you describe the atmosphere of your workplace? Is it welcoming? How would you describe its culture? Is there a hierarchy of relationships or only one of roles?

- Consider the changes that you would like to make to improve your institution's environment, atmosphere or routine.

Chapter 8

Focus on you

In the last chapter, we looked at the atmosphere, structure and routines of an organisation, and considered the profound positive effect that values consciousness can have on its life and work. In this chapter, we will consider your role in the process of becoming values-based.

At a presentation I was giving at Ferndale School (in Swindon), a teacher was sitting in front of me who had a constant smile which seemed to light up the room. By the middle of the afternoon, I couldn't resist asking her what was making her feel so cheerful. She confided that she was deliriously happy because she had just got married. It may be a challenge to maintain such euphoria, but how do we care for ourselves so that we can maintain a positive demeanour? A question: Do you suffer from TBD? These initials stand for Too Busy Disorder. My experience of hearing responses to this question makes me think that you probably think that you are too busy. Many people feel that they have become human doings rather than human beings.

One of the biggest current health concerns is mental health. Large numbers of individuals feel that they are stressed and take medication to help them cope with life. Stress turns up the volume of our sensitivity and may lead to unacceptable behaviour such as road rage. You may have been the recipient of someone who becomes angry and threatening to you because you have made a driving error. I witnessed a scene outside our local pharmacy, when an elderly man was trying to park his car between two others. He was taking his time and finding the process difficult. A line of traffic built up as he manoeuvred. Eventually the car was successfully parked. However, as the traffic began to flow, the driver of a white van gesticulated with his hand and shouted a crude obscenity at the man. He looked visibly shaken as he got out of his car, but was comforted by the woman who stands outside the chemist selling the *Big Issue*, and who is a local landmark.

I understand that people who are on the receiving end of road rage take longer to calm down than the perpetrators of this unacceptable behaviour, partly because the body is drenched with adrenalin – the fight-or-flight chemical. I suggested to a group of early years teachers in London that they cut out pieces of card in the shape of circles, and ask their children to colour them in as smiley faces. The teachers were then to attach a short length of cane to each smiley face and give one to each member of staff to be kept in their cars. When they were next on the receiving end of road rage, they could hold up their smiley face, which would help them to remain calm and hopefully help the road-rager to see the funny side of life.

Gill Ellis, an innovative values-based head teacher at Coed Eva Primary School (in Wales), also uses humour to tackle stress in her school. In the office, she has placed a notice that has the title 'Stress Reduction'. There is a black circle on the poster in which is written in bold, 'Bang head here'. Underneath the circle are the following instructions: 1) Place on firm surface. 2) Follow instructions in the circle. 3) Repeat step 2 as necessary or until unconscious. 4) If unconscious stop stress reduction activity. More seriously, Gill and her associate, Nicola Morgan, have written a wonderful teaching programme called 'Family Values', which is an excellent resource for helping families to invest in values and take care of each other.

Two questions that are rarely asked in any organisation of its employees are: How do you look after yourself? and How do we look after each other? Please pause and ask yourself how you look after yourself. What sort of things do you do?

Pause ...

Answers I have often been given include, 'I walk the dog', 'I go to the gym', ' I meet with friends', 'I go to bed early', 'I read a good novel' and 'I reach for the gin bottle!' It surprises me that so few of us really employ what I heard the Dalai Lama refer to as 'wise selfishness' – understanding that we must care for ourselves so that we can then effectively care for others. The Vietnamese writer Thich Nhat Hanh states that, 'The practice of a teacher or any helping professional should be directed towards him or herself first, because if the helper is unhappy, he or she cannot help others' (Hanh, 1975).

At the start of my headship of West Kidlington School, I encouraged the staff to think about ways that would encourage us to take more care of each other and ourselves. One of our ideas was to introduce massage for any staff member who wanted it. We asked a wonderful masseuse, Carlo, to bring her portable massage table to school on a regular basis and at the end of the teaching day to give a massage to those who wanted it. Carlo's sessions became very popular with staff who claimed that it made a positive difference to them. I remember an amusing incident involving Carlo and an Ofsted inspector called Maurice, who was part of a team inspecting the school. I recall Maurice scurrying past me in the corridor on his way to observe a lesson. He suddenly stopped in his tracks and turned to speak to me. He hurriedly said, 'I hear you do massage here. If it is a part of the school, then I think that I should inspect it by having one!' I managed to hold back my mirth and told him that I would ask Carlo. I did and she said, with a glint in her eye and gesticulating with a wringing of the hands motion, 'What part of his anatomy do you want massaged?' Humour is a great stress reducer!

Many schools have adopted massage both for adults and pupils as a way of reducing stress levels. At Ledbury Primary School (in Herefordshire), head teacher Julie Rees has introduced pupils to peer massage. I have watched the progression of this work from Year 2 to 6 as children learn both the caring protocol and benefits of the experience. Julie says that it is an important element that underpins her values-based school. Nudge Symonds, head teacher at West Kidlington, works in a similar way with yoga, employing an expert during teachers' planning, preparation and assessment time. At other primary schools, I have seen music and movement sessions, such as 'wake and shake', that create a positive mental attitude in staff and pupils. In secondary schools, I have watched intuitive teachers, such as Alison Clark, when she was working at Bartholomew Secondary School (in Eynsham), still their classes with reflection activities, thereby creating a calm and relaxed atmosphere (more on this in Chapter 10). Taking time to think about how we care for each other and ourselves leads to well-being and happy staff. Our immune system is strengthened, and there is less absenteeism through illness and therefore, from an economic perspective, fewer lost teaching days.

A question: What, in the last few months, has been your *wow* factor? What experience has made you feel *wow?*' Just think about this for a moment and let your mind reflect on what has given you a sense of joy.

Pause ...

I have been amazed at the answers I have received to this question. The majority of people talk about wows like this: 'My wow was seeing my daughter get a medal at the gymnastics competition. You see, I was filled with joy, tears streaming down my face because she had recently recovered from leukaemia'; 'It was when my boyfriend looked so lovingly into my eyes and asked me to marry him'; or 'My son Bertie playing football and being voted the man of the match'. During my presentations, I have never heard anybody say things like, 'My wow was using my new iPad!' Wows are usually about features of our relationships with others. We are relational beings and we get the most joy from others. The converse is that, when relationships are not in harmony, they cause us emotional pain. Schools which deliberately focus on creating and maintaining good relationships are more likely to create a positive culture, where both adults and students enjoy being together.

A suggestion: if there is someone at your place of work or at home with whom you harbour any negative feelings, then do something to repair or enhance that relationship. Remember though to ensure congruency between your social and psychological message. It is always the psychological message that is heard, so if you say, 'Hi, it's good to see you', but you don't mean it, then the person will know. I expect you will have experienced this at social gatherings when a stranger approaches you and asks about what you do for a living, but you feel that they aren't really interested. Another way of expressing this is that it is always important for our values to be aligned with our behaviour, otherwise we lack authenticity.

My wife Jane, a psychotherapist, and I have developed what we have termed 'the inner curriculum', which is about the knowledge and skills that help people in education to develop a strong and secure sense of self. We think that a working knowledge of transactional analysis helps adults and students to develop the key skills of self-awareness and an understanding of others. Such knowledge supports personal, positive self-change, which people who want to be values-based need to possess. We have worked with school leaders over several years giving them insights into values, transactional analysis and mindfulness to support them as they develop values-based schools. David Linsell, head teacher of Ratton Secondary School (in Eastbourne), says that a focus on values-based education has had a profound effect on his school:

> By developing a common understanding of what our values mean we have grown together as a school. By using our values as a common point of reference for all we do, values have brought much greater cohesion to a large, complex and diverse organisation. At Ratton, good people (staff and students) follow our values; great people encourage others to follow our values.

As a result, many more of our community see themselves as leaders and all are clear about what behaviours are acceptable and why.

On transactional analysis, David says:

Developing an understanding of transactional analysis has helped us to sustain good relationships and manage stress in difficult situations. Seeing oneself as the adult in the room, and understanding why others are not, has enhanced professionalism and empathy. It has enabled people to predict and understand behaviours in difficult situations, and as a result enhanced self-confidence.

Jane recommends that educators and students can deepen their self-understanding through the use of the transactional analysis model developed by its originator Eric Berne. Transactional analysis practitioners, such as Julie Hay (1995), have taken Berne's work and developed useful tools, such as 'windows on the world', which enable us to gain invaluable insights into our own behaviour. In this model, we are invited to look at the world through a window that has four panes of glass. Each pane represents a way of viewing the world, three of them with a negative bias but one representing the life stance, 'I'm OK and you're OK'. So many of life's relationships fail because we don't have a positive attitude about ourselves and/or others.

As parents, we can fall into many parenting traps. My friend Andrew Fuller, clinical psychologist and author of *Tricky Kids* (2007), reminds us to use language that can help shape behaviour. He suggests that parents use 'I noticed' feedback for positive and negative behaviours. Comments made to adolescents by parents that begin with the phrase, 'I noticed …' can powerfully shape their behaviour. For example, 'I noticed you are really trying hard to …' or 'I noticed you're reading a good book'. Adults can use this to calmly draw attention to negative behaviours. For example, 'I notice you are up when you are supposed to be asleep' or 'I notice that you are feeling upset right now'. Andrew believes that this gives young people a chance to explain their actions or comply with parents' wishes. If you're a parent or teacher, try it!

Cath Woodall, head teacher at Revoe School (in Blackpool) says, 'It's what's in the minds and hearts of the adults that count.' This is why adults need to be self-aware and mindful about the potential effects that our words and actions have on others. The starting point for self-awareness is valuing and caring for your self, which is what I heard the Dalai Lama refer to at a conference in Scotland as wise selfishness. If we fail to care for ourselves, we become sick or unable to keep a sense of proportion when life is challenging. A simple yet profound method of reminding ourselves about important truths is to recite mantras. Here's one for you to say out loud now:

I am lovable and capable.

From my experience, people often fear that they are not lovable and capable, with the result that they limit their potential because they have low self-esteem. I have worked with gifted adolescents who, despite impressive exam grades, are convinced that they are failures. They lack self-belief. A values-based family, school or other institution creates a social climate in which individuals are helped to recognise and nurture their intrinsic human qualities.

A young friend of mine, Nicola, who is a dedicated and enthusiastic primary school teacher of younger children, shared with me a story about herself that is an example of how we can be over-sensitive and upset by the behaviour of others and, as a result, suffer from afflictive emotions (e.g. sadness, frustration, anger). Nicola recalls a particular Friday when she'd had a great teaching day in every respect. All her activities with the children had gone well and at break times it hadn't rained and there was no wind (which can make children over-active).

At the end of the day, she was in the cloakroom helping her pupils get ready to go home. There was a buzz of excitement as the children were saying goodbye to each other. During this process, Nicola looked up and, on glancing out of the window, noticed one of her children's parents, Mrs Jones, marching purposefully across the playground towards her. As Nicola went into the playground to dismiss the children, Mrs Jones, without any preliminaries, said aggressively, 'Why hasn't my

Warren changed his reading book this week?' Nicola's heart dropped as she fumbled for an answer. In that moment, she was speechless. Mrs Jones continued her tirade and then with a final, 'Make sure it doesn't happen in the future', marched off with a sullen Warren in tow. At home that evening, Nicola told her husband Mark that she'd had a really terrible day. Had she? The next day, she felt depressed and was consumed with thoughts about Mrs Jones. On the Sunday night, she confided to Mark that she wasn't looking forward to returning to school the next day and was wondering why she was a teacher. Mark did his best to console her and to lift her spirits – with little effect.

On the Monday, Nicola arrived at school having slept badly and figuratively beaten herself up all weekend. She was on early morning playground duty when who came striding towards her but Mrs Jones. Without hesitation, Mrs Jones said, 'I've come to say sorry. You see my husband wound me up and I was in a foul mood last Friday. Warren says that you are a good teacher and parents say you are too. Warren also said that you did change his book, but he had left it in his bag and didn't tell me.' With that, she left! Nicola had allowed herself to be upset for a whole weekend for no good reason.

Does this story resonate with your experience? It certainly does with mine. We will all react to this in different ways, depending on our personalities and life experience. Some may think that Nicola shouldn't have been so sensitive, but in my experience teachers try to please others and they care – that is one of the main reasons why they become teachers – and they consequently take to heart negative comments from colleagues, parents and government. Remembering our *wow* moments at such times of crises can help, as is remembering that we cannot be responsible for the emotions and actions of others. The inner curriculum teaches us how to be in control of our internal world so that we can respond appropriately to others without damaging our sense of self.

In Chapter 10, I suggest elements of reflective practice that would have helped Nicola to manage her distress, but in the next chapter we will focus on the crucial importance of good relationships as an integral part of values-based education.

Some reflection points to ponder from this chapter:

- What changes are you going to make to ensure that you care for yourself?

- How are you going to encourage people at your place of work to care more for each other?

- What are you going to do to develop your own inner curriculum?

Chapter 9

Focus on your relationships

In Chapter 8, we put the focus on ourselves, recognising the central importance of self-awareness and inner stability. In this chapter, we will continue the theme but put the focus on our relationships.

In this regard, the person who comes immediately to my mind is Michael Antoine, the head teacher of Praslin Secondary School (in the Seychelles). Michael is a determined, values-based leader, who is conscious about the importance of nourishing good relationships in his school. I have watched him as he has talked to staff, students and parents, and observed his many excellent qualities. He constantly maintains good relationships with staff and students, whilst giving positive leadership and holding people to account for their actions. He understands that good relationships are crucial to the development of a values-based family and school. In his school can be seen the development of a vital ingredient of a values-based school, *relational trust*, which is an outcome of good parenting, teaching and friendship. This quality operates between individuals and develops when we feel unconditionally valued for who we are as people.

Another principal who embodies positive values and has the natural ability to foster relational trust is Paul Daley, principal of Sancta Maria College (in Auckland). In my view, Paul is an exceptional leader and has a significant influence not only in the life of his college, but on the direction of education in New Zealand. One of Paul's engaging qualities is an endearingly dry sense of humour. There is a story about him that one day he was working at his desk in his office. The room has reflective windows through which he can observe students during break times, but they can't see him. All they can see is the reflection of themselves. Paul was sitting at his desk when a Year 7 boy came to the window near where he was sitting and started looking at himself as he combed his hair. Paul observed this for a moment and, with a glint in his eye, decided to slide the window open and speak to the student, who he thought would be amazed to see him. After a moment's hesitation, with the two just looking at each other, the boy coolly said, 'Could I have fries with that order, please!' Paul dissolved in laughter at this comical situation. Four years later, he remembered this event and asked his personal assistant to buy a small portion of fries. The teacher on break duty was asked to arrange for the student to come up to Paul's window, not knowing why. When Paul saw him standing there, with a flourish he opened the window and said, 'Sir, here are your fries, sorry the order took so long!' This story wonderfully demonstrates relational trust in action, and the vital importance of humour and fun.

Another example: Julie Carr is the head teacher of Lyneham Primary School (in Wiltshire). RAF Lyneham closed in December 2012 and, alongside Royal Wootton Bassett, has sadly become known for the repatriation of soldiers killed in Iraq and Afghanistan. Julie's school largely for caters for the children of forces families. She does an incredible job to create a climate for learning that is relational and supportive of the families in her community. Because of troop movements, the school can have a turnover of a third or more pupils during any one year as soldiers come and go. She has found that, by developing a values-based school with a focus on quality teaching and relationships, the staff team can quickly gain the trust of the children, families and community.

On one of my visits to the school, Julie was giving me a tour and we were discussing the developments that had taken place and how the staff had been working hard to develop excellent practice. It was towards the end of the school day and we were passing a classroom when a Year 1 boy came bursting out with a note in his hand and a broad smile on his face. Julie crouched down to speak to him at eye level and the boy pushed the note into her hand. She opened it, gave the boy a huge hug and said how much she appreciated him. We passed on and, after a few moments, I asked Julie what had been written on the note. She somewhat reluctantly told me that it had said, 'Mrs Carr, I love you very much'.

I would like to share with you one last story that powerfully illustrates the importance of relational trust. It features a student and teacher whom I observed at the Regis School, an 11–18 Secondary School in West Sussex. A little background: David Jones is the head teacher of the school. I first knew David when he was a colleague head at Gosford Secondary School (in Kidlington) and was interested in the values work at West Kidlington School. On moving to Bognor Regis, he started on the journey of developing values-based education in this coastal secondary school with 1,400 students. The school is proud that it is pursuing Rights Respecting School status, in which the United Nations Convention on the Rights of the Child sits at the heart of the school's planning, policies, practice and ethos.

David began the school's values journey by consulting widely with the key stakeholders of staff, students and parents. David says:

> Not surprisingly, there was a significant degree of consensus about the core values, although the interpretation of what is deemed a 'value' was varied. For our students, it was about respect, trust, honesty, enjoyment and a sense of humour. Our parents cited respect, support and care. For the staff team, the focus was on respect, trust, positivity, aspirations, a sense of humour and consistency. The consultation was important in that it allowed all parties to give voice to what was important to them.

David is a head who leads by example and consensus. He told me that the school made respect its core value and staff realised that, to embed sustained improvement, they had to model it in all their dealings with students and the wider community.

David invited me to the school to audit how values were being embedded in the behaviours of staff and general routines. At 8.45 a.m., after attending a staff briefing, I was walking along one of the school's corridors, observing the start of the teaching day, when a student came charging along. She had obviously lost her temper and was using language that would make a soldier blush! She pushed past me and was soon taken to one side by a member of staff who skilfully began the process of calming her down. The day passed, and I was delighted to see the improvements that had been put in place and the enthusiasm of the staff for the values agenda.

For the last lesson of the day, I found myself in what the school refers to as the Ozone Support Centre – where students who find life and school difficult spend time in a nurturing environment. I soon noticed the girl I had seen earlier in the day, but this time she was in quiet conversation with the teacher in charge of the unit. They obviously had a very positive relationship – their body language said it all. Their smiles lit up the room. When the student moved back to her place, I went up to her to see if she would chat with me. As I approached, she looked up and fixed me with a stare before saying, 'Oh, you're the man I knocked into in the corridor this morning. Sorry, I was off the wall and feeling *very* angry. If you had my home life, you would be angry too!'

She showed me the project work she was working on, which she said was helping her to develop her personal and social skills. Finally she said, 'My teacher here is great. She never loses it with me and I feel safe with her.' What I had observed was the value of respect, which David and his staff had decided to make their focus, being lived in the school. The outcome was a great example of relational trust. My assumption is that the girl in this story was not experiencing the effects of relational trust in her family.

My understanding is that the development of relational trust is ideally an outcome of good parenting, the process beginning with the very young child. One morning, I watched as my son-in-law, Simon, prepared breakfast for Sophie, my then two-year-old grandchild. He was involving Sophie in the process by asking her to go to the fridge and fetch her milk. She went to the fridge and said, 'Here's my milk. It's the purple one. That's my favourite.' Sophie was referring to the purple-coloured top on the plastic milk container.

What I noticed was Simon's patience and how, in this simple process, he was involving Sophie and reinforcing his positive relationship with her. Simon is an early years teacher who understands the developmental needs of young children and the importance of setting clear boundaries that create safe and secure relationships. He demonstrates the truth that teachers – like the ones in the stories above, who are able to connect and have positive relationships – have the most effect on student progress and achievement.

Values are contained in ourselves, in our words and through the relationships that we have with others. We first learn about values in our relationships with our parents and prime carers. Concerns are currently being expressed about the growing proportion of young children – the 'looked-after' generation – who spend so much time with a range of strangers in childcare that they are not forming the necessary strong attachments and relationships with their family. As a consequence, the values and behaviours that are being encouraged are not necessarily those of the parents.

Economic imperatives have placed a need for many mothers of young children to work, not by choice, but by necessity; members of my own family have voiced their concerns about this fiscal pressure. Government policies, such as conditions on maternity pay, have encouraged their early return to work without, in my view, adequately considering the developmental needs of very young children – safe, loving and secure attachment. This situation makes it even more important that adults in early years settings, such as nurseries, are positive role models for the growing numbers of children who need to be able to form good relationships.

I saw a brilliant example of this when I visited the Forrest School, a new purpose-built pre-school near Skövde (in Sweden). The high adult-to-child ratio, the design of the building and the obvious qualities that the adults demonstrate make it a very happy place for children to experience positive values. In Iceland, the principal of Leikskolinn Alfaheidi, Valgerður Knútsdóttir (Valla), showed me in her values-based pre-school how the staff's first priority was to establish loving and meaningful relationships with the children. The school's assembly was a testimony to this, as staff and children interacted naturally as would a caring family. No artificial distance was created in the school between adults and children, yet even the youngest children behaved responsibly. This was a wonderful example of adults consistently modelling the chosen values of the school's community, with Valla demonstrating, through her leadership, the alignment of her personal values with her behaviour. All the policies and routines followed in the school were also in alignment with the school's espoused values.

I have never been in a good school that does not generally have good relationships. Relationships need constant, active attention and cannot be taken for granted. May I suggest that if there is someone in your life, perhaps a colleague at work, with whom you find it difficult to form a good relationship, then take the responsibility to begin the process of relationship building. It may not be easy, but it will demonstrate that you are living your values.

We can also find ourselves misunderstood. For instance, leaders, such as head teachers, who walk about schools too distracted by their internal worries to acknowledge others, soon find that difficulties arise in relationships, as staff perceive that they are being ignored. Remember that a values-based school or institution is by definition and foundation a relational establishment.

In the school context, good relationships act as the glue between the school curriculum and personal dispositions, thereby allowing students to flourish in school life. Human beings are generally social beings, and I believe that it is through good relationships that we find meaning, purpose, happiness and contentment in our lives. This is why relationships act as the very bedrock of a values-based institution or community.

Some reflection points to ponder from this chapter:

- Spend a few minutes thinking about how you are developing relational trust in your relationships. Think about this in the contexts of home and work, and consider some appropriate actions to enhance your relationships.

- Open, honest and empathic communication underpins good relationships. How could you improve work or family routines to improve relationships (e.g. regular (in the diary) family meetings to check how everyone is thinking and feeling about their lives together)?

- Remember that good relationships begin with the relationship you have with yourself. Give time for you!

Chapter 10

Focus on adopting reflective practices

In Chapter 1, I invited us to be in relationship on our journey through this book. I am hoping that, by this stage of your reading, you feel connected to both what I am writing about and me; that you sense my meaning and purpose, which is to inspire others to adopt and work with positive, universal, human values. May I reiterate again that, as you introduce and develop the 10Fs of VbE (see page 75), you do so concurrently, as all are of equal importance.

As I sit at home beginning this chapter, I feel a real sense of excitement. This is because I am about to share with you the transformational element of what Jane, my wife, and I have termed the inner curriculum of values-based education. This is the skill of *reflection*, which I define as follows:

Reflection is the ability to access our internal world of thoughts and feelings, and to regulate them, which helps us to sustain mental health and increases our capacity for self-determination.

A little personal history: on becoming head of West Kidlington School in 1993, I began to introduce reflection into the curriculum as an integral part of values-based education. For many years previously, I had noticed that people who appeared to be reflective seemed to be more self-aware and have a greater capacity for wisdom.

A notable example of this was the late Dr John Williams, the chief education officer of the Isle of Wight Education Service. In my then role as principal adviser, John was my boss, but also so much more than that as he was a shining example of a brilliant role model. His capacity for reflective-led behaviour gave him the capacity and wisdom to steer the education service during challenging times of restructure and uncertainty. I witnessed the centrality of reflective practice in being an effective leader, so it seemed natural that my interest in this topic should expand when I returned to lead a school as its head teacher.

In introducing reflective practices to staff and pupils in the early 1990s, I was acutely aware of the potential for controversy. At that time, if you had been a parent of one of my pupils, what would you have thought if you had heard that the school was introducing meditation? The word *meditation* can be emotive and was then, despite its place in all major faiths, generally linked with the practices of Eastern religions. I was therefore acutely aware that its practice could be open to being misunderstood in the context of a British state school. It was not my intention to deceive, but I didn't want an unfamiliar term to lead to an inaccurate perception about what we were instilling in the children.

My aim was to demonstrate to the school community that reflective practices were the missing link in education's search to raise academic standards, and to enable children to develop holistically as creative, knowledgeable and civil people. I was aware of other less emotive synonyms such as *silent sitting* and *reflection,* so I chose the term reflection as, for me, it fully encompassed the empowering techniques that I wanted to encourage. I need not have feared, because I soon gained the support of the local Church of England curate, Sue Boyes, who occasionally spoke at school assemblies. Also, when author and journalist Frances Farrer wrote her thought-provoking book about the school's work, *A Quiet Revolution* (2000), the then Archbishop of Canterbury, Rowan Williams, wrote a commendation.

My caution had been ill-founded as reflection was gradually gaining the support and attention of the community in general. Also, the school was being increasingly visited by a range of international visitors, keen to understand its values practices, particularly reflection, and – the subject of the next chapter – its *ethical vocabulary.* By the late 1990s, with the profound developments in neurobiology, I was beginning to source evidence from the scientific community to support the work I had been pioneering. This support has continued and, in the last five years, human brain research, notably the work of Dr Daniel Siegel and associates in the United States, is demonstrating the positive outcomes of developing reflective practices. Dan and I both refer to reflection as the fourth R – Reading, Writing, Arithmetic and Reflection – to stress its importance in the curriculum.

I would like to ask you to pause in your reading and picture your best friend on the screen of your mind.

Pause ...

I don't know whose image or essence you have brought to mind. What you did was to trigger that part of your brain involved with memory – you reflected. I suspect that you didn't think of yourself when I asked the question! However, we spend all of our time with ourselves and share only some time with others, yet we don't normally consider ourselves to be our best friend. Why? I think that sitting with yourself in silent reflection should be like sitting with your best friend – *you*. It builds the essential personal powers of self-control and self-confidence.

To begin to understand the gentle power of reflection, we need to practise it, so I am now going to invite you to have an experience of reflection. If you are currently in a noisy place that might distract you, then move to somewhere more conducive to being still and silent. If you are already skilled in the practice, then you will be aware that you can access the benefits of reflection wherever you are.

Before we start, a health warning. If you are currently going through a particularly difficult time in your life, perhaps you have recently been bereaved, then during the following exercise be mindful of keeping the essence of you safe by not dwelling on any disturbing thoughts that may arise. I recall a time when I led a reflection for teachers in training at Rolle College (in Exmouth) and a student came up to me afterwards to say that her father, who had died, had been in her thoughts during the reflective activity. She said, however, that she wasn't upset because the image of him had been accompanied by a profound feeling of peace.

You will probably find the following exercise easier if you read through all seven steps first, so that you understand the process before beginning your reflection. The exercise is called *pausing to be*. When I lead the exercise during a presentation, I time a minute exactly using my wristwatch, but if you are alone, you will have to guess at the time or perhaps set an alarm on your phone. Try the exercise and then read my commentary on its potential benefits.

Pausing to be

1 May I invite you to feel comfortable where you are sitting. No need to adopt a special sitting position, but ensure that your legs and arms remain uncrossed and that your body feels comfortable and relaxed.

2 Find a place to rest the gaze of your eyes. Some people prefer to close their eyes, but you may find that if you do this your brain may sense that you want to go to sleep!

3 Now, slowly take in a few deep breaths – imagine that you are taking in clean mountain air – and feel relaxed. Let your shoulders relax.

4 When you are ready, sit for about a minute just being aware of your thoughts and feelings. Don't judge them or try to control them; merely observe them.

5 When the minute has passed, then move your body and bring your consciousness back to the place in which you are sitting.

6 Now pause and consider what you have just experienced.

7 Make *pausing to be* a daily habit.

At this point, I would really welcome being able to share your experience with you. I have conducted this exercise many times and I am always fascinated by the reactions it provokes. Here are some typical ones:

… Isn't a minute a long time?

… I wanted the minute to go on and on.

… My mind started making to-do lists.

… I realised that I am not my thoughts but I was observing them.

… I found trying to be still irritating.

… I became aware of all the sounds in the room.

… For the first time in ages I felt peaceful.

… I seemed to let go of thoughts and ground myself in who I really am.

So what are the potential benefits of this activity? I was talking with a friend, a medical doctor who practices reflection, and he said that when most people start pausing to be, their breathing and heart rate slow down, and there is a tendency for blood pressure to lower slightly. When we become practised in the technique, our thoughts appear to slow down too and we have a greater sense of personal control and well-being – our attitude is more calm and positive.

Consider, just before the moment when you cease this earthly existence, do you want to say that you have done a lot or been a lot; that is, have you been fully present in your life and not just occupied with endless activity? I think most of us would opt for the former.

Will the technique help you to be both a happier person and more effective in your role at work? I am convinced that it can. Let me share with you how pausing to be can help in practice. I shall describe two scenarios that I hope will illustrate the importance of reflection. They both feature the same teacher, but there is a difference.

Scenario one

It is a wet Friday afternoon, the first lesson in an inner city secondary school. Jim, a proficient languages teacher, is teaching a challenging Year 9 group. In the last lesson he has a Year 7 group, known in the school as a great group to teach, as they are all so eager to learn. The Year 9 lesson has got off to a bad start with low-level disruptive behaviour. The group is not in the mood to learn, and Jim is forced to draw on all his teaching and behaviour management skills to keep order and their attention. The lesson drains him and, by its end, he feels angry and stressed.

The end of lesson is signalled and Jim wastes no time in getting to the Year 7 group who are quietly waiting for him in another teaching block. Without thinking, Jim, red-faced and anxious, bursts into the room and without hesitation says, 'Now hear this, I'm not standing for any nonsense!' The students look at him perplexed and Jim feels foolish, as he remembers that this is a great group to teach and will be hanging on his every word. The lesson goes reasonably well, but he goes home for the weekend feeling generally drained by his day.

The second scenario again features Jim and the same two classes. This time Jim has been trained in reflective practices so his awareness is different.

Scenario two

The Year 9 class is challenging, but Jim keeps his professional integrity and is emotionally detached from the behaviour of the students. The students see that he is remaining calm and dealing with their behaviour appropriately, whilst maintaining positive relationships. Nevertheless, by the end of the lesson, Jim feels that he is in need of pausing to be to ground himself before he teaches the Year 7 class.

After the Year 9 group leave the classroom, Jim remains and sits on a chair for one minute, withdrawing into his internal world. He is well practised in the technique, and quickly feels both grounded and energised. On entering the Year 7 class, he says, 'Wow, I have been really looking forward to teaching you today. I have a fun lesson prepared so that we can have a great end to our week.' The class beam at Jim as they respect him as a brilliant teacher and man. Jim goes home having enjoyed his week at school.

I recommend pausing to be at least three times a day. It is a regular habit of mine; for instance, I pause to be before getting out of my car, before meetings and after them, prior to giving a presentation and often during one when the audience is engaged in group discussion. Sometimes, when folk say that they haven't got time to practise it, I suggest that a possible solution is to add an extra minute to the time when they are visiting the toilet! I recommend that you encourage all meetings to start with pausing to be. Also, if a meeting seems to be straying from the agenda and is becoming unproductive, then invite everyone to be still for a minute and then continue the meeting – it's amazing the effect such a seemingly simple practice can have on ensuring positivity and productivity.

The difficulty is often not in pausing to be but in remembering to do it. It has to be habituated so that it becomes second nature. For most of us, it is counter-cultural and our brains reject it as a waste of time. To make it become a habit, we need to practise it for thirty days, after which it will become second nature. During the thirty days, set up reminders to pause to be. It is easier if there is a culture at your work that sees reflective practice as a 'normal' part of life. If you remain unconvinced about the economic, personal and social benefits of reflective practice, then please read *Presence*, the insightful book by Peter Senge, Otto Scharmer, Joseph Jaworski and Betty Sue Flowers (2004), or Otto Scharmer's incredible work entitled *Theory U* (2009).

Once you have seen the benefits of pausing to be you may catch the reflection bug as Jane, my wife, has done. She sets her morning alarm so that she wakes half an hour before she needs to get up. On waking, she has this time to be in reflection. She begins this process by focusing her attention on her breathing. When her thoughts wander, she returns her attention to her breathing. This simple activity strengthens the neural pathways of her brain that give her greater awareness and self-control. She says: 'What I noticed is that I have gained a greater control over my emotions, which has helped me choose my responses to others more appropriately. It has also enhanced my capacity to think through problems and scenarios creatively. My colleagues have seen a new quality in me that they are intrigued by – they want some of it!'

By now you may be wondering why I think reflection is so important for us to practise. You will be aware that, in this chapter, I have been discussing reflection in the context of a skill that we, as adults, need to develop. I am also aware that if we are not convinced of its benefits then we will not stress its importance to children. If we don't practise it, then we will find it difficult to teach and model to others. So what are the benefits of reflection? There is a growing body of scientific research that has identified the outcome measures of reflective practice. According to Dr Daniel Siegel, these are generally the same outcomes that are found in good parenting. Dan's work has identified nine measures, which you can read about in his book, *The Mindful Brain* (2007).

Jane and I have been giving demonstration lessons in schools on what is called *mindsight* – the ability to see one's own mind and sense those of others. We have found that children are fascinated to learn about the functions of their brain and the effect that reflection has on the part known as the prefrontal cortex. The school curriculum generally focuses on facts, knowledge and skills related to the outside world, a material world that encourages children to concentrate their relationships on external objects – the *external curriculum*. Conversely, reflection focuses attention on the internal world of the brain and puts the spotlight on our relationship with our self and others – *the internal curriculum*.

I think that schools need to have a balance of both these domains. One such school is Addison Primary School (in London). Its head teacher, Pete Dunmall, has understood the benefits of reflective practice and has introduced mindsight as a part of the school's values-based curriculum. Pete says:

> Mindsight gives children the tools to better understand and manage their emotions and behaviours, helps them to become calm, and increases their empathy and a sense of optimism. Taught sessions, where we visually represent current research in cognitive neuroscience, enables children to develop a framework for learning about self-awareness, while simple activities help children sharpen their ability to focus attention and build self-regulation skills. The impact of this work boosts children's social and emotional competencies, and helps create a more optimistic classroom. Children tell us things like, 'Mindful breathing makes me calm and helps me to concentrate.'

Reflection transforms the brain by developing the neural connections in the prefrontal cortex. In *The Mindful Brain*, Daniel Siegel suggests that it also develops the following qualities:

- Self-awareness and the ability to direct our thoughts
- Resilience
- Social and emotional intelligence
- Emotional control
- Ability to pause and reflect on consequences before taking action
- Understanding our adaptive behaviour and making positive changes
- Compassion
- Empathy
- Academic success
- A deepening sense of morality

In a phrase, *we expand and deepen our level of consciousness.*

I hope that I have inspired you to experiment with reflection as a personal tool for nourishing your internal world. If you already regularly practise reflection, then I would like to suggest that you deepen and expand your daily experience. By so doing, you will be able to model the practice to your children if you are a parent, or to your pupils if you are a teacher. I believe that it is important to teach children about reflection and how to do it from an early age. I have observed early years teachers enabling their children to reflect by building their capacity to sit still in silence.

At Ledbury Primary School (in Herefordshire), I observed a creative teacher who had asked her pupils to sit still on the carpet as she tried to distract them by blowing coloured bubbles at them. The children were determined not to reach out for the bubbles, as young children are inclined to do! Some schools set aside rooms or areas of the school, such as gardens, as tranquillity zones. These areas support reflection as a mainstream activity in the school.

I have also seen teachers using visualisation techniques to support the process of developing the capacity to reflect. Simon Poote, a teacher at Long Crendon Primary School (in Buckinghamshire), says: 'We need to get the children to slow down a bit, because they live busy lives with lots of distractions. If we can get the children to calm their thoughts, then they are more able to listen, which helps them with their learning.' He suggests simple ways of understanding their minds to his pupils. Simon's wife, also a teacher, created the following exercise:

> Imagine your thoughts in your head, which are like a busy motorway … thoughts going backwards and forwards … lots and lots of thoughts, like lots and lots of fast cars. How can we slow down our thoughts and take out unnecessary ones? Now imagine that you are sitting on a country gate watching the peaceful scene as a slow tractor comes rumbling along. Let your mind be like this peaceful country lane …

With older pupils, video can be used to grab their attention and help them to understand the purpose of reflection. For instance, in the film *Kung Fu Panda* (2008), there is a wonderful scene where Po the Panda is over-eating and feels very upset because he isn't being successful in his quest. The wise old tortoise, Oogway, arrives on the scene and, after listening to Po's distress and confusion, tells him not to worry about what has been or what is to come. He says, 'Yesterday is history, tomorrow is a mystery, but today is a gift, that is why we call it the present.'

Expanding our capacity to live in the present is a beneficial outcome of reflection. *Mindfulness* has become a popular term for describing a range of ways for focusing our thoughts in the present moment. Pausing to be is a mindfulness technique, and you will recall how my wife, Jane, begins silent reflection by focusing her attention on her breath. Each time her mind wanders onto other thoughts, she brings her attention gently back to her breath. May I invite you to create time for your pupils to practise this regularly, because science is showing that such a simple, yet difficult, activity strengthens the neural pathways of the brain that aid concentration and personal control.

Reflection can be used during any lesson. I watched a secondary school science teacher ask his class to stop their work, be still and reflect about what they were trying to achieve in the session. The quality of the lesson improved because of this pause. Another example featured a humanities teacher, Alison Clarke, who had given her Year 11 students pieces of spiral-shaped pasta and asked them to look closely at each part of the spiral and, whilst observing, to reflect about why some people in the world were at the bottom of the spiral with very little, whilst others were at the top with so much. The richness of the debate that ensued, in terms of reasoning, was greatly enhanced by this reflective time.

Increasingly teachers are being supported in their efforts to develop reflective practices in the classroom. The Catholic Diocese of Melbourne has produced a DVD to help teachers to develop meditation in their classes. Dr Michael Downey, an experienced teacher, is the director of formation at Loreto College (in Brisbane). I asked him what he had learned by teaching reflection. He said:

> I have learned that if I start a lesson without a moment of still-ness, then what I am about to teach them is just one more drop in an already over-full cup and I am gambling with the potential success of this lesson. When I do begin with stillness, it gives all of us a chance to catch up to ourselves before our lesson begins. That is how we make sure we are all ready to begin to encounter and engage the subject matter waiting for us.
>
> In one school, I took a Year 9 class in the last two lessons after lunch on Fridays. The class was challenging at the best of times, but not only was this lesson on Friday afternoon, when they thought that their main priority was preparing for the weekend, but their double lesson before lunch was sport. In other words, for these students, school finished with morning break on Friday.
>
> In an exercise of unbridled hope and optimism, I began each Friday afternoon with them with a centring exercise and silent meditation. Initially, the silence was a struggle and, being Year 9 boys, the opportunity to 'let rip' with wind in the silence proved too much of a temptation for some. I persisted, because quite quickly both they and I seemed to settle into a slightly calmer place to begin our lesson. I also found that immediately after our meditation we could speak to, and hear, each other more clearly and, surprisingly, by the end of term, we actually liked each other and our two minutes of silence had grown to seven min-utes or more.

You may wonder what Mike's pupils think about him and his values-based style of teaching. This is what one student wrote: 'While in your class, we never felt wrong or stupid or inadequate or like you were talk-ing to us because it was your job. We never felt judged in your classroom. You seemed to look at us in a different light, like you didn't see another bunch of kids, but people with potential and this changed the way many of us see ourselves.' I think you will agree that this is a wonderful comment about the power of a values-driven teacher as a positive force for transformation.

As I bring this chapter to a conclusion, I would like to give the last word on the importance of reflection to someone who uses and teaches it, but who does not work as a teacher in a school. Floyd Woodrow takes values-based education into business environments through his company, Chrysalis. Floyd had a distinguished career as a member of the Special Air Services and has written a seminal book (with Simon Acland) on leadership called *Elite!* (2012). Floyd has trained some of the top British athletes and has profoundly influenced the leadership development of companies such as British Telecom. I asked Floyd what reflection meant to him and this is what he said:

> Reflection is a skill I wish I had learned a long time ago. It has helped me to understand what is going on in my mind … my thoughts, feelings and situations that affect me emotionally. What's more, how I can be in control of them and direct them. It has helped me with my awareness of others and myself … with the teams I work with … I understand what I need to do to have better rapport, better communication, being able to respond to what's happening in the now. It has also helped me to understand who I am from a values perspective. Do I do these things that I talk about to others? Have I the correct behaviours? Am I authentic in what I do? We have to go internal to think about that. For me, reflection has given me the gift of communication.

Wow! I think Floyd's testimony helps us to recognise the importance of reflection in every walk of life. I hope that you are now enthused to engage with reflective techniques, such as pausing to be, and that you can sense the benefits and bring them into your own life. I am on record as saying that reflection is the most important skill to teach in the twenty-first century, as it is an integral part of developing and deepening understanding about universal, positive human values. It gives us a greater capacity to reflect on the deeper meanings of the words that make up the values vocabulary, which is the subject of the next chapter.

Some reflection points to ponder from this chapter:

- Think about my definition of the term *reflection* at the beginning of the chapter. How currently do you maintain your own mental health?

- Set yourself up with a daily routine for pausing to be. Keep a journal describing what you notice about yourself as you embed the practice. Ask others if they notice any differences about you.

- What are you going to do to help others – such as your own family, your work colleagues or your pupils at school – develop reflection?

Chapter 11

Focus on an ethical vocabulary

In Chapter 1, I mentioned that in the 1990s, whilst head of West Kidlington School, I was part of a small group of students who were admitted to Oxford University to undertake doctoral research, whilst continuing their professional career. I had the privilege to have as my supervisor and mentor Professor Richard Pring, who was the renowned director of the Department of Education. Richard's keen intellect guided a transformational research project, which took ten years to complete, that looked at the effects of introducing values-based education into schools. The core of the research considered the effects of introducing an ethical vocabulary (values words) to pupils.

In Chapter 6, you will recall that we considered the process involved in selecting a group of universal, positive human values. The outcome was to gain the general agreement and commitment to a deliberate and systematic consideration of the meaning of the values words. This examination helps in the development of what I have defined as *ethical intelligence*, which I think is the ability to be *values conscious*. Such self-awareness gives us an insight into our thoughts and actions, and the actions of others.

Deliberate and systematic values education enhances values consciousness. For instance, parents, students and teachers develop an increased consciousness about the meaning of values, and the power of values education to transform learning and life. In our home, Jane and I choose a value each month to think about. We secure the word with a magnet in a simple display on the fridge as a daily reminder. Throughout the month, we consider the many layers of meaning that the word has and, in reflection, consider how we are living the value in our lives.

At an organisational level, such as a school, it is crucial to establish and then consistently use a common and shared values language in every aspect of the institution's life and work. It is the power of this shared language that creates the positive transformational culture of the school.

There are two aspects of the values vocabulary: the *explicit* and the *implicit*. The values words are explicitly taught during a strategically planned learning programme of experiential lessons, assemblies and themed events, so that pupils have a deepening understanding of their meaning as they progress through the year groups of the school. They are taught implicitly through a common shared language. For instance, you may observe two pupils playing harmoniously during break time and say to them, 'I noticed you playing so cooperatively, well done!' Or during a lesson, 'You all showed such respect for each other's thoughts and work.'

I recommend that all adults in the school are involved in developing the values vocabulary. For instance, support staff at lunchtimes can praise pupils for using values. A practical way of doing this is to have a display of glass jars, each labelled with one of the school's values. Children who display a value whilst playing can be invited to place a coloured glass bead in the appropriate value jar. As the jars fill up, it can be seen which of the values are being used the most in the school. It's a fun way to highlight values and keeps the vocabulary in the forefront of consciousness.

A values school is a can-do school, focusing on the positive. Kathy Wood is the head teacher of Hornbill School (in Brunei). Hornbill is a British school for the children of mainly service personnel, predominantly Nepali, who are stationed in the country. I have visited this excellent, creative and values-based school twice and was enthralled by the richness and depth of its curriculum, with its focus on a creative, enquiry-led curriculum. The school ably demonstrates how to get beneath the surface of values-based education, and really embed the explicit and implicit aspects of the values vocabulary. Hornbill

School's quality of curriculum and exceptional leadership is apparent in Kathy's observations:

> The challenge for us was to find answers to the question of how we were going to really dig beneath the surface, on both the explicit and implicit aspects of values for life, so that anyone who walks through our school door can feel it at work instantly. It has to permeate everything we do.
>
> We did not want our values provision to be at a superficial level where, say, we devoured one pineapple chunk at a time or tackled one piece of a much bigger jigsaw, piece by piece. We wanted to make sure we had a unique, highly textured experience to offer, so that all who had contact with our school would know values had made a difference to us; we in turn had made a difference for or to them.
>
> To do this, we reviewed our provision through the senses, so that children and staff (and visitors) could actually feel and touch values in action; they could see it at work everywhere they went; they could hear and smell it. The spoken word promoted it in everyday conversations and, most importantly, from all of this there is an emotive, spiritual response that is created and lived.
>
> As head teacher, it is important to be constantly identifying with values for life, and what this means for you as an individual and for the school in which you lead. Trust and communication are two elements that must be addressed in a practical way from the outset and revisited regularly. Without seeking a deeper understanding of these two critical elements and how they impact on the running of a school, values education becomes meaningless in the context in which we work. Having a collective understanding of what values really mean in action and context has helped us to overcome the many hurdles we face in effective school provision and leadership today.

Values for us are everywhere in our school environment and in our 'being'. Each day, we remember we can all smile in the same language and we do!

Kathy's point about seeking a 'deeper understanding' of values is crucial. Values-based education is not merely about putting some values words on the classroom wall and thinking that the school is now values-based. It is about carefully planned and structured experiential lessons, which ensure that pupils are active learners, experiencing, thinking about and engaging with values so that they can live them in every aspect of their lives.

Children need to be able to relate the vocabulary to real-life situations. A brilliant example of this happened during a formal school inspection by Ofsted at Washingborough Academy (in Lincolnshire). As part of a curriculum theme on 'African Adventure', the academy was delighted to have been able to establish e-mail contact with a school in Namibia. During the introduction to the lesson, Sandra Mitchell, the deputy head, had showed the children the actual e-mail from the African school and broke the news to them that the academy's ICT technician had set up a blog to enable them to keep in contact with the school.

The children were buzzing with excitement and keen to notify the Namibian schoolchildren all about their own lives in Washingborough. As a result, Sandra led a circle time session and asked the children to consider what impression they would want to give of Washingborough Academy to a school in another country. She told me that she had imagined that the children would start telling her all about the academy's 'Bike It' days, the wonderful new library or the amazing school grounds, but she was completely overwhelmed when the children instead said that they would like the Namibian school to know about their values education, to show that they respected people and appreciated their points of view.

One particular child very thoughtfully commented: 'We need to consider the feelings of the Namibian children,' adding that, 'We should be modest about what we actually talk about, as we would not want to brag about all of the things that we have, in case they have nothing!'

Other children, when questioned about what they could offer as a partnership, then went on to say that they should hold a sponsored event to support the Namibian school, in order to buy any resources that they might need. Sandra said afterwards:

> Having experienced this sensitivity and thoughtfulness on a daily basis, I was not overly surprised by the children's contributions. However, the observing Ofsted inspector commented on how moved she was by the children's comments; she stated that this had proved that not only did we say we 'covered' the values at Washingborough Academy, it was obvious that we actually lived the values.

The inspector was duly impressed by the way the pupils both used the values vocabulary and lived them. The final inspection report highlighted the positive effects of the academy's values in the curriculum. The school was rated outstanding for pupil behaviour based on its values-based education.

In another outstanding values-based school, Ledbury Primary (in Herefordshire), I watched the values vocabulary being considered at a very deep level as part of a philosophy for children (P4C) lesson. The Year 6 pupils had been divided into groups of six, each being given a pack of values cards. On each card was written the name of one of the school's adopted values. The teacher asked the children to display the cards in a shape that would show the values that they thought were most and least important.

What impressed me during this lesson was the quality of discussion about the meaning of the words. The pupils really did understand what a value is (a principle that guides our thinking and behaviour) and what they mean for the way we should live our lives. Some pupils thought that respect was the most important; others thought that honesty was and so on. I remember a tingle going down my spine when one girl said, 'I think love is the most important, because if you don't have love, you can't have any of the others.'

Julie Rees is the head teacher of Ledbury School and is passionate about values-based education. Her delightful book, the *Little Book of Values* (Duckworth, 2009), is a wonderful resource for primary schools that want to develop values-based education. She believes that introducing the richness of the values vocabulary has had an incredible effect on the school:

> Adopting and embedding VbE at Ledbury Primary School has given staff and pupils a common vision and ethos for living and learning together. On a daily basis, a values vocabulary is applied throughout the school, both in the classroom and during extra-curricular activities. It gives pupils a common vocabulary to use with peers and staff. Pupils are encouraged to explore the meaning of the vocabulary through philosophy lessons and teachers' planning incorporates cross-curricular links to use a values vocabulary. The pupils develop a maturity of thinking and show that they can empathise from a very early age as a result of developing this vocabulary.

The values vocabulary is displayed throughout Ledbury School. Many primary schools choose twenty-two values, one a month in a two-year cycle. Over the six years of primary education, a child revisits a value three times, in a spiral curriculum, each time at greater depth and understanding. The value of the month is displayed in the school hall, as featured at Eardisley Primary School (in Herefordshire), with head teacher Bridget Knight.

Bridget says that the school's consistent focus on values grows a spirit of joy in the school; they are more than words on a wall.

> Joy is much underrated in the current education system – but joy is potent; joy is powerful. Joy creates an unparalleled atmosphere that sustains emotional and spiritual flourishing and academic focus. There's more to values than just 'having val-

ues'. In fact, there's a world of difference. Values that are just a backdrop, a word on a wall, remain just that or, at best, express an unfulfilled hope ... Values that are enacted, lived, discussed, debated, wrestled with, loved and enjoyed, stimulate the heart and the mind and build the very ground from which our approach to life springs and flourishes. Our children feel the difference. They talk about knowing and feeling they are valued – and in turn they freely value others and themselves. They are in no doubt about the value of values.

At Eardisley, the current value word is also prominently displayed in every classroom, the school's reception/office and in the head teacher's room. It is on letterheads and mentioned in newsletters with examples of how the value can be developed at home. Teacher Rebecca Rees wrote to me enthusiastically, saying:

Since starting at Eardisley I am constantly re-evaluating my teaching pedagogy and my overall attitude so as to encompass the school's positivity. Values-based education has taught me to look more positively at situations that I might have otherwise dealt with differently. It has also taught me to take time, reflect and consider situations before acting. I am understanding the value and power of silence and I am also feeling more comfortable in allowing myself time to be reflective. I am striving to create a calm, happy and positive learning environment in my classroom. In doing so, I can see a marked change in the attitude of the pupils in my class.

All the school's values are referred to on a daily basis, as I also witnessed at Greenfield Lower School (in Bedfordshire). A Year 4 class had been engaged in a cooking session, making simple but yummy cakes. At the end of the session, the teacher asked the children which values they had used to make the lesson successful. The pupils showed that they really understood the school's values vocabulary as they talked about the cooperation, respect, care and patience that they had used. It is good practice to make clear the learning intention for a lesson, but I would suggest that the values intention is also made clear and that this is reviewed in the plenary part of the lesson.

In secondary schools, such as Ratton School (in Eastbourne), the values vocabulary is evident around the building. Ratton displays its core values on quality posters. The head teacher, David Linsell, has a picture of what he describes as the Ratton Bus on his office door. On the bus, the school's values are displayed: respect, integrity, excellence, enjoyment and participation. Whenever David is interviewing new staff, he asks them, 'Are you on our values bus?'

I was impressed at Ratton to see the values vocabulary being implicitly used across the curriculum. For instance, values were evident in a skilfully crafted ethics lesson with Year 10, which had as its focus the moral efficacy of fertility treatments. The open and honest discussion of moral dilemmas is an important aspect of the values curriculum for adolescents. It gives them the opportunity to talk about difficult social and moral issues, away from the environment of playground peer pressure. Also, in a drama lesson with Year 9, I witnessed the use of the school's values in a creative session that was helping students to understand the power of body language and emotions.

In another outstanding values-led secondary school, Aylestone School (in Hereford), the care of students is very evident in the way the school caters for new students if they arrive during an academic year. On arrival at the school, a student is placed in the Learning Centre for a few days and given time to find out about the school, and for the school to assess the new student's needs. The student adjusts to the school's values culture through a carefully constructed induction programme.

A student told me that the induction programme had made a big difference to her as she had been made to feel so welcome in the school. She had feared just being taken to a form room to be met with a sea of new faces. At Aylestone, she was able to make a few really good relationships with staff in the Learning Centre, so that she gained in confidence before being introduced to her form. This is a school where the values vocabulary can be seen in action in all aspects of the school's life. Head teacher Sue Woodrow says:

> Having been head teacher of three secondary schools in challenging circumstances over the past ten years, two being placed by Ofsted in special measures and one teetering on the brink, there has never really been for me any meaningful alternative to approaching the whole issue of school improvement by building relationships first and foremost. When organisations, and therefore individuals, are under immense pressure, the highest standards of behaviour towards one another are absolutely vital.
>
> Meeting Neil Hawkes, I realised that we shared a passion for this guiding principle. Neil has been a mentor and advocate, offering help and guidance. His method of articulating his all-important philosophy of values-based education, with its focus on developing an ethical vocabulary to improve provision, outcomes and quality of life for children and all who work in schools, immediately resonated with my own experiences and has remained a touchstone for me throughout my career as a head teacher.
>
> VbE is so needed in the English schools' climate of relentless accountability and measurement. The challenge we face is to value each other and hold each other to the highest standards of behaviour – to be the best people we can be – whilst challenging and supporting our students to the highest possible academic, creative, sporting and artistic achievement. A tough job, but a job worth doing.

My experience of values-based education in action convinces me that values have the power to change lives. I often use an emotionally poignant short video by www.purplefeather.co.uk to underline this point. It features a blind man in Glasgow who is sitting on a pavement with a notice that states: I am blind. People pass by and occasionally put a coin or two in his collecting tin. A young lady approaches him (I am convinced that she went to a values school!) and, after pausing, picks up the man's notice, turns it over and, after writing on it, moves on. Passers-by now start giving generously to the blind man and, when the young lady returns, he has been given a lot of money. Sensing her presence, he asks, 'What did you do to my sign?' She replies, 'I wrote the same but different words.' The sign now reads: It's a beautiful day and I can't see it.

The point is that, if we alter our words and make them more positive, we can change the world. The subtle power of the values vocabulary has the potential to lead to the cultural transformation of families, schools, businesses and, yes, countries too!

Some reflection points to ponder from this chapter:

- Experiment at home by having a monthly value to think about. Display it on your fridge using a fridge magnet.

- Deepen your own understanding of a values vocabulary by exploring the meanings of words such as respect, tolerance and compassion. It helps if you are able to share what you have found with others.

- What actions will you take to develop a values vocabulary in your work setting?

Chapter 12

Focus on being a role model for values

In the previous chapter, we looked at how values-based education introduces and develops an ethical vocabulary of values words, which becomes our moral compass. For instance, when words such as *courage* are explored, we realise that it is a concept that sits between the two extremes of *cowardice* and *foolhardiness*. If the value of courage becomes a part of who we are, shown in our behaviour, then it can be described as one of our virtues. I find it helpful to define a virtue as a value in action.

I would like to invite you to pause and reflect about a value that you consider is a part of you and shown in your behaviour.

Pause ...

I wonder which value you have been thinking about? I too paused in my writing and I was thinking about the value of friendship. This is our current family value, which is displayed on our fridge at home, and we have been thinking and talking about how we show this quality. Are we keeping in regular contact with our close friends? How do we display friendship to strangers? Are we a good role model for this value? Do we have sufficient awareness to know what we are modelling through our body language? Are we as friendly as we think we are? Is our behaviour sometimes outside of our conscious awareness? Do we see ourselves as others see us? I find the most challenging aspect of values-based education is to model accurately the values that I espouse.

Are you a perfect human being? Relax, you don't have to be perfect. Being values-based does not imply that we must think ourselves to be somehow without flaws. What it means is that we acknowledge our humanity, but also that we are on a journey of self-improvement and are doing our best. A challenge for a values-based institution is when, as in all human organisations, things go wrong and mistakes are made. If a guiding value is not humility, then people outside the organisation will be quick to tell you that you say you are values based, but in practice you aren't.

I have always enjoyed the *Fawlty Towers* series on television featuring John Cleese as Basil Fawlty. For me, the brilliance of this sitcom is linked to John's ability to exaggerate human behaviour. I suspect that I laugh, as many do, at his bizarre conduct, because I can catch myself displaying similar, if not so exaggerated, traits. There is one particular scene that comes to mind when Basil is driving his small red car and it breaks down. He gets uncontrollably angry and shouts, 'Start, you vicious bastard! … I'll count to three. One, two, three. Right, that's it! You've tried it on just once too often! … I'm going to give you a damn good thrashing!' He gets out of the car, fetches a branch and proceeds to beat the car with it. No one would argue that Basil is a good role model! But perhaps we see glimpses of ourselves in his behaviour.

What then constitutes being a good role model? I recall observing Mike, an early years teacher, greeting the pupils in his class as they arrived. In this school, parents/carers are asked to bring their children into the classroom when they drop them off at school. As the pupils arrived, Mike crouched down to their eye level. With a twinkle in his eye and a broad smile, he welcomed each one personally and shared a brief conversation. I could see that the children loved this meet-and-greet routine, which acted as a bridge between home and school. The parents knew that this was designed to be a special time for their child and teacher, and not a time for them to have the teacher's attention. The class assistant was on hand to take any messages that parents had for Mike or to arrange a convenient time for them to talk with him.

As I observed Mike, I was aware of his being a great role model for the children. I realised that being a role model for children means being the sort of person you hope they will want to become. We show them the adults that the world needs them to be. We model what it is to be a values-based human being. How we model this will, to a large degree, determine what a child thinks they should grow up to be. This is why I consider that parents, and also adults who work in schools, are very important for the creation of a civil society. They are in the forefront of positive, cultural transformation. In turn, the children become role models too. At the Meads Primary School (in Luton), an eight-year-old girl proudly approached me holding a silver cup in her hands. Beaming with pride, she said, 'I've been given this cup, because I'm the class role model of the week.'

Role modelling is also given a high priority in values-based secondary schools worldwide. For instance, at Seaford High School (Australia), Praslin Secondary School (Seychelles), Helenaskolan (Sweden) and Sancta Maria College (New Zealand), I have witnessed outstanding examples of students acting as role models for their peers. In these schools, the psychological distance between adults and students is much closer, whilst accepting the difference in roles, than I often see in schools that are not so relational, humane and explicitly values-based.

At Helenaskolan (in Skövde), students and staff have open discussions about the organisation of the school. On visiting the rektor, Tobias Axnemon, to see how the school was embedding values, he arranged a meeting of students to talk about what they were doing. In fluent English, they answered questions and also wanted to hear about ways they could develop the school still further. It was evident that the student voice was taken seriously and that staff/student relationships were excellent.

One of the most challenging aspects of being a values-based institution is not so much the selection of values, but the conversation that ensues about behaviours that will model the values. For instance, what should we do more of, or stop doing, if we promote the value of respect? What would be your suggestions in the context of your workplace?

I have had some robust conversations with staff in schools when they have tried to set down what they will stop doing. In one school, a member of staff suggested that, as a consequence of adopting the value of respect, it would no longer be OK for any adult to shout at a student. This brought a quick response from a teacher that he had always shouted at students, and that this was the way he gained and maintained respect. This comment opened up a lively and, at times, tense debate about the school's preferred culture, its vision and aspirations for the future. A member of the senior leadership team asked, in a non-confrontational way, whether the school wanted, in terms of its pedagogy and practices, to be in the twenty-first century. The majority of staff thought that, in order for them to receive respect, then it had to be appropriately modelled and therefore shouting was inappropriate in most circumstances.

I hope this example helps you to understand that a discussion about values and behaviours touches people deeply, but gives a real opportunity to determine the principles that will create the climate for learning and the school's or company's culture. I sum up a values-based culture as one that is calm and purposeful, and where there is mutual respect. The purpose of an open and honest discussion about staff behaviour is to achieve consensus so that there will be consistency in the school. For students to take the school's values seriously, they need to feel that each member of staff will treat them according to the school's values.

Occasionally, I am unable to present a school with the International Values Education Trust's Quality Mark because there is inconsistency in staff behaviour. Once the whole staff reaches an agreement about how members will model the values, then the school can describe its values and behaviours in its documentation. An example from the UK would be Ledbury Primary School which has declared itself to be a 'no shouting' school. Some schools have written these agreements into job descriptions and in information for applicants for teaching and non-teaching positions.

Another poignant example of the impact on culture of staff modelling values can be seen at Woodland Middle School, a school in Bedfordshire for pupils aged between nine and thirteen. Jeff Conquest, the head teacher, says:

> Introducing a values-based culture into our school was a decision that we made to deliberately alter our school's ethos. We wanted to effect a change from one where many staff acted as poor role models to one where they modelled and radiated good values for children to reflect back.
>
> The values-based approach within our school now permeates our practices, behaviours, policies and decision-making, and, importantly, the changes that we wanted to see in others, we now see in ourselves. The result of being more mindful of displaying values in all our interactions (between staff, pupils, parents and visitors) is that the school's ethos has warmth that is palpable and a genuine synergy between all the stakeholders exists.

What Jeff says emphasises the need for each one of us to take the lead in modelling positive human values. Often this is not an easy task, but there are tangible rewards in terms of the affirming culture that is created.

Some reflection points to ponder from this chapter:

- Choose a value and make a list of the ways that you are going to model it. Note in your diary a month hence when you will review your progress.

- Get some feedback from your family or work colleagues about the values that they see you modelling. Do you have an accurate picture about the effects on others of your behaviour?

- Remember that it is more likely that others will form an impression about you because of your behaviour (what you model) than from what you say.

Chapter 13

Focus on school assemblies

As we have journeyed together through the pages of this book, I have shared with you what I call the three pillars of values-based education: the values vocabulary, reflective practice and authentic modelling. These three come together as a powerful values cocktail when used in school assemblies. If you are not a teacher in the British tradition, you may be unfamiliar with the term *school assembly*.

To explain: a school assembly occurs when the whole school, or a part of it, comes together to focus on what the community considers is of worth. Assemblies have been enshrined in various legal Education Acts in England since 1944, mainly to ensure that collective acts of religious worship are held in schools. In many other countries, pupils are gathered together for an assembly. However, countries such as the United States have taken legal steps to prevent religion being a part of state education and therefore schools rarely have times when staff and pupils gather together for an assembly. Please allow me to sidestep the pros and cons of having a religious perspective in assemblies, as it is not a focus of this book. I am sure that you will have your own views, depending on your religious or cultural background.

During my time as a head teacher, I found that school assemblies powerfully established the school's ethos of being calm and purposeful, and were vitally important for the transmission of school culture, values and vision; that is, who we are, what we do and where we are going. The coming together as a school community creates the opportunity to celebrate and feel part of a larger body of people. My aim, as head teacher of West Kidlington School, was to ensure that assemblies inspired listeners, both staff and pupils, to want to be better people. I therefore deliberately devoted a great deal of my time and thought to the creation of quality assemblies that helped the community to celebrate being a values-based school. Frances Farrer gave a detailed account of the format and content of these assemblies in her insightful book, *A Quiet Revolution* (2000).

A high quality school assembly, whether religious or secular, nurtures a climate that stresses care and valuing of the self and others, as well as the pursuit of excellence. During a successful assembly, pupils tune in and can have spiritually awakening experiences. Assemblies become a very positive occurrence, once their influence and impact, to both individuals and the school in general, is truly recognised and understood. They profoundly foster the development of emotional intelligence and spirituality. In this context, I define spirituality as that which is concerned with the inner personal world of thoughts, feelings and emotions. I am sure that you would like to know how values-based school assemblies can be structured and organised, so in this chapter I hope to give you an insight that will help you to see why assemblies are an important ingredient in values-based education.

As mentioned in Chapter 6, in many values-based primary schools the academic year is structured around twenty-two values (eleven each year on a two-year cycle). This means that, each month, the focus for school life and assemblies can be based around one of these values. I would like to stress this is just one effective model among many and that it is important to create an assembly pattern that fits into the context of the school. For instance, some secondary schools choose to focus their assemblies on fewer values words to gain greater depth in understanding the concepts that the words convey.

Here's an example taken from part of a school's assembly schedule in England:

Date Week beginning	Value	Theme
6 September	Respect	What are values?
13 September		Religious ceremonies
20 September		Prayer/reflection
27 September	Honesty	Famous people
4 October		Health week (Care for Yourself)
11 October		Aspects of Hinduism
18 October		Harvest
1 November	Peace	Remembrance: discussion about conflict – prayer for peace
8 November		Jesus
15 November		Feelings/thoughts
22 November		Worship
29 November	Happiness	Individual differences
6 December		Positive attitudes/ character/personality
13 December		Christmas

You can see in this example that the school has a weekly theme, sometimes of a religious nature because of legal requirements in England, but that this specific focus is taught in the context of a monthly value. I should stress that the chosen themes need to reflect the social and particular religious or humanistic background of the school (e.g. Christian, Hindu, Jewish, Muslim or non-religious).

Whatever the context, I recommend that thought is given to the environment in which the assembly takes place. The physical setting is important in creating the right atmosphere. Here are some ideas for a school assembly in a school hall (although I am aware that, in some countries, assemblies also happen in the open air):

● Create a central focus, such as a display to encourage pupils to think about the theme of the assembly.

● Use music to create a calm and reflective mood.

● Consider using blackout, spot lighting (if available) and a good sound system to help make assembly a special time.

● Use computer presentations to project reflective images for the pupils and staff to see when entering assembly (e.g. a beautiful natural scene).

● Ensure that everyone can hear who is speaking.

● At the start of the assembly, as the pupils arrive, its leader should be seated in a calm attitude, appropriate for a reflective experience.

● All adults model the behaviour that is expected of the pupils.

● Ensure that pupils are actively included in all aspects of the assembly.

● Use high quality stories; these can be based on personal experiences.

Good planning is vital, as last minute assemblies do not often provide meaningful experiences. Assemblies that are planned around one of the school's values can be discussed and considered in the classroom by teachers. This is why many schools like the values cycle, because pupils' thoughts and ideas can be explored back in class as part of legitimate curriculum time.

I wonder what you would expect to see during a values-based assembly? Pause for a moment to picture what you would envisage experiencing.

Pause ...

I'd love to be able to discuss with you what your expectations are! Compare your own ideas with the following assembly case study that features a school that I know well – West Kidlington School. I took this photograph of Eugene Symonds, the head teacher, just before the start of the school's morning assembly.

You will notice that Eugene is relaxed, happy and seated. As the children entered the school hall, he made eye contact with them. The adults allowed the children to seat themselves and they sat at the side, modelling the behaviour that they were expecting from the children. The assembly actually started in the classrooms and the pupils were encouraged to come to assembly in a reflective calm mood. Calming music was played and there was a relaxed and purposeful atmosphere.

On the day I visited the school, the value that was being thought about was unity. Eugene involved the children in an amusing, lively, thought-provoking experience as he helped them to understand the concept. Eugene is an inspirational, authentic role model who, on this occasion, demonstrated how unity is seen throughout the school. We were helped to think about the concept of unity by considering the way good relationships are developed and how the school works together to achieve high standards. The assembly involved the singing of the rousing school values song 'Look to the Future', written by Linda Heppenstall, a much respected former member of the school's teaching staff. I recommend that primary schools write or adopt a values song that all will enjoy singing.

Eugene has ensured that assemblies are seen as an integral and carefully structured part of school life, which play a central part in the school's values-based learning. He says:

> At our school, assemblies are the most important event of the week. They enable our school community to gather in a climate of calm reflectiveness. Pupils and adults focus on refining their understanding of values and how this can support their academic, social, moral and spiritual welfare. Through carefully structured approaches, assemblies support the principle of providing regular opportunities to gain greater understanding of values-based learning. They are often fun but never just entertainment. They have key messages that we invite children to take away inside their hearts. Children tell us that they are important for them too, which is why we work so hard on them. Attendance at assemblies by children and staff is prioritised, as they are as much about informing and reminding adults as they are about providing guidance for children. They are a time when the whole school community can consolidate what we want to achieve through values-led learning.

What I noticed, and found moving, at West Kidlington was the ability of the pupils to be still and focus their attention. This is no accident, as the school has taught reflective practices for many years, so it is quite natural for staff and pupils to respond appropriately when invited to reflect about what the assembly meant for them.

Reflection at the school is a time of silent sitting, when pupils are invited to be still and simply be. The person leading the reflection may ask questions in order to help guide pupils' thoughts. During this time, the children focus on positive aspects of themselves, others and the world (see Chapter 10 for details about reflection). Reflection is an effective contributor to raising feelings of self-worth and enables people to take responsibility for themselves.

Values-based assemblies have other benefits too, which can include:

- Heightened awareness of the needs of others.

- Greater sensitivity to the feelings of others.

- Raised self-esteem.

- Good behaviour based on self-discipline/self-awareness.

- Potential to heighten consciousness.

- Development of spiritual, social and emotional intelligence.

- Generating a school ethos that is calm, happy and purposeful.

- Raising achievement and standards.

- Contributing to developing personal autonomy and contentment.

- Staff and pupils perceiving that assemblies are worthwhile.

Finally in this chapter, I would like to stress the importance of enabling young people to be active participants in the learning process in an assembly rather than being passive recipients. I have seen some excellent assemblies where pupils have been actively involved and engaged in a deep learning process, the result being that young people have told me how much they enjoy taking part in school assemblies.

For instance, at Aylestone Secondary School (in Hereford), I watched an outstanding assembly with Year 10 students when our hearts and minds were touched as a teacher talked intimately about the value of care, sharing with us her sadness about the recent death of her dog. The intensity of the silence in the school hall was almost overwhelming as the teacher shared her feelings with us. Students were invited to talk about their experiences too. The intimacy of this discussion and the way students responded to it showed the respect that the teacher had for the students and vice versa.

I hope that in this chapter you have sensed my conviction about the importance of the school assembly as an essential vehicle for values-based education. The school assembly has the potential to establish and maintain a culture that inspires the school community to focus on the value of quality in every aspect of its life.

Some reflection points to ponder from this chapter:

- If you are a parent with a child at school, do you know what happens at the school's assembly? Ask your child or perhaps, if invited, take the opportunity to attend one.

- If you are a teacher or support member of staff, how do you feel about assembly? Is it a time you enjoy and feel nourished and enriched by attending? What contribution could you make to improve the experience of assemblies?

- If you are a head teacher or principal, what do you do to ensure that assemblies are a highlight of the school day or week for the school community?

Chapter 14

Focus on the school's curriculum and its leadership

In this chapter, we will consider the vital role of leadership and the school curriculum in values-based education. If you are not a teacher, you may not be familiar with the word *curriculum*. For me, the curriculum is everything that happens in the school. It therefore includes both what is planned and intended, such as lessons, and what is informal and unintended, such as playground relationships. Values-based schools deliberately underpin all aspects of the curriculum with universal, positive human values. I am sure that you now fully appreciate that values-based education is not a separate subject, but a way of conceptualising education that invites us to ensure that our behaviour stems from a desire to live life based on a powerful set of universally regarded values.

From my experience of supporting the development of many schools, I have seen that values-based education is only successful in schools where the head teacher or principal is fully committed to its principles and practices. This is because the leader of the school is primarily responsible for its values, vision, culture, philosophy and practice. They are also aware that past leaders have an effect on the school's current culture. A challenging question for leaders to consider is the extent to which they have created or inherited the culture and, if the latter, have they acquiesced to it? The leader's influence is paramount, and they must be prepared and trusted to act as the key, authentic role model for values-based education. Trust is the key value here because, in my experience, the higher the level of trust in an organisation, the more successful it becomes. This is because all staff and students are watching the leader's behaviour and judging its genuineness; that is, can I trust him or her?

How can the leader be an authentic role model for values-based education? I think that a key to achieving this is the leader's ability to manage both their internal and external worlds in a consistent and cohesive way, so that they attain, maintain and enhance their internal stability and external equilibrium. I believe that this is more likely to be achieved if we regularly stop, experience stillness for a short time and connect to our grounded self, in order to be calm and centred. In the terms of transactional analysis, we connect to our grounded adult ego state – the person we are when we like ourselves the most. Good leadership is leading from the inside out, so that what we think and feel is seen in our actions and behaviour. To have this capacity of congruency requires us to ask the sometimes uncomfortable question: Why do I say, and do, what I do? Being prepared to understand who we are, and the processes underpinning our behaviour, results in greater consciousness. Consciousness is awareness with a purpose. The purpose is always to act from our espoused values and remain grounded in them.

I sense that a leader is more likely to be grounded if there is an appreciation of the influence that their personal story has had on their sense of self and how this understanding influences their decision-making. Therefore, to learn effectively and act with integrity, leaders, as well as students, need to connect to the influence of their internal worlds. Consequently, the values-based leader has to model this insightful understanding to all other adults and students.

Developing a shared and common values language – understanding what values drive our thinking and behaviour – is essential for the leadership of any school, business or country. For example, understanding and applying values, such as equality, justice, fairness, transparency and openness, is crucial, as I believe they act as ethical guides for the values-based leader if they are going to be trusted. Such an understanding enables leaders, who are values-based, to face challenging circumstances, because they develop a stable personal internal world based on integrity, resilience and altruism – the servant leader.

Once the leader is convinced and committed to being a values-based leader, then the senior leadership team of the school need to be inspired to understand the philosophy and practices of values-based education, and be empowered to support him or her. One of these individuals may be delegated with the responsibility for being the curriculum leader for values-based education. I am reminded of Jason O'Rourke, who I first met when he was deputy head teacher of Hornbill School (in Brunei). He had been given responsibility for curriculum development and I remember him showing me a series of labelled boxes, which contained materials to support the various aspects of the school's enquiry-based curriculum. I was impressed that values permeated all aspects of the school's teaching and learning. Here is Jason and his boxes.

Values-based education permeates all curriculum subjects. Professor Mick Waters, formerly director of curriculum at the Qualifications and Curriculum Authority (QCA), draws attention to the way that the curriculum encompasses the whole experience of learning in a values-led curriculum primary school in Herefordshire in his book *Thinking Allowed: On Schooling* (2013). Also, at Sancta Maria College (in New Zealand), I witnessed the school's values across the curriculum. For instance, in the learning support department, I saw excellent student–staff relationships enabling students to learn from an active, experiential curriculum that supported students' individual needs. At Snells Beach Primary (also in New Zealand), I was enthralled to see values embedded in the school's skills-based active curriculum. On a visit to

Ascension Kindergarten (in Singapore), I witnessed parents visiting the school during their lunch breaks to experience active learning with their children (as in the photo above).

Parents told me that the sessions help them to understand the school's curriculum and find out about ways that they can support learning with their children. The values of cooperation and mutual respect were very evident in this creative values-based environment. The principal, Dianne Seet, explained to me that the school was encouraging fathers, in particular, to come into school to learn with their children, which she thought was helping men to understand how young children learn best. She was keen that they find out how to support their children, in a way that fosters the understanding of key learning principles. All these schools make values-based education an integrated curriculum concept, rather than a programme, an event or an addition to the curriculum. They develop relevant and engaging values approaches, connected to local and global contexts, which offer real opportunity for student agency.

Agency is a term that describes the capacity of individuals to work independently, make ethical choices and act on them. Values-based education strengthens pupil agency when it involves various forms of giving, outreach and working in the community; for instance, through values action projects that allow pupils to enact their values. Agency is developed through meaningful real-life experiential learning, such as engagement in community projects, when there is an opportunity for the development of initiative and leadership, and an explicit focus on ethical, intercultural and social issues. For instance, at Madley Primary School (in Herefordshire), I observed groups of Year 6 pupils who had set up mini businesses in order to understand all the things that are needed to make them successful. To make it especially meaningful, local firms had agreed to link with the groups so they could have first-hand experience of the business world. In the lesson I was observing, the pupils were deciding on the values that they thought should be the pillars of their businesses, the teacher having introduced the concept of business ethics to them. They discussed the need for cooperation with other companies, trust in their bank and respect for all the people who worked in the business. Whilst watching this outstanding and thought-provoking lesson, I speculated that many real-life businesses would benefit from having similar discussions.

How would you teach young children to understand the value of trust? Young children learn best through first-hand experience, so what activity would embed the understanding of this value in them? Here is one solution suggested by Long Crendon Primary School (in Buckinghamshire).

The photograph shows a Year 2 child carefully guiding a blind-folded Year 1 child over an obstacle course. When the picture was taken, the teacher was saying, 'Good trusting Molly', and the boy was being encouraged to think about the words he was giving as directions, because Molly couldn't see him pointing – a great learning experience for them both.

In a Year 8 class at Ratton Secondary School (in Eastbourne), I watched spellbound as an exceptionally talented drama teacher unpacked key values underlying good interpersonal relationships through the medium of role play. His energy and enthusiasm inspired students to step outside of their own inhibitions and enter safely into the perceived worlds of others. Such meaningful experiences rarely happen by chance, but are outcomes of good teaching and good planning.

I saw an outstanding example of this when I was conducting a values audit for the International Values Education Trust's Quality Mark at Beenham Primary School (in Berkshire). A number of years before, the head teacher of Beenham School, Sue Butcher, had worked with me when she was a teacher in Oxford. At the time, the school in which she was working was facing challenging circumstances and I was asked by the education authority to give leadership support. I was head teacher of West Kidlington School and was pleased to share the success of values-based education with this school. In Sue I soon recognised a person with integrity, whose espoused values were in alignment with her behaviour. This congruence was seen in her patience and consistency of behaviour when dealing with pupils.

When I visited Sue in her current school, I saw that she was modelling these qualities to staff and pupils by creating a calm and purposeful ethos in her school assembly. What was also exciting was the way that she and the staff had embedded values in the curriculum and the pupils were actively involved in their learning. For instance, the assembly was both reflective and active. An element of the assembly consisted of the children forming groups in the hall to discuss what should constitute the elements of a peace garden in the school. Leadership of the groups was initially given to certain pupils and then, after a time, the groups were asked to delegate the leadership role to someone else in the group. The children were learning about the importance and benefits of distributive leadership. Adults were asked by Sue to be observers of the groups, only helping when the process needed it. Sue told me that the result of making pupils take more responsibility and become more active in the curriculum was that standards had improved significantly. High expectations and the ability to listen deeply were also factors that I believe have contributed to this school's positive relationships and high academic standards.

At Beenham, the pupils understand what they are learning. They have a common language for learning which includes the values vocabulary. This was illustrated when a Year 5 pupil said, 'I am not drowning in my learning today because I am consolidating it. I am using the value of resilience to remind me to persevere.' An outstanding values lesson with Year 5 and 6 pupils had as its learning intention 'to recognise the gifts that we can share with others'. The lesson helped the children to identify the gifts that they should share with others and to determine the gifts that make the biggest impact. By the end of the lesson, they had decided that non-material gifts, such as friendship, were the most important.

I asked the teacher if she would show me where the lesson fitted into the school's medium-term topic plan, as I sensed that the school was giving a lot of thought to embedding values deeply into the curriculum. The planning sheet showed how the school was developing an active learning-based curriculum and the values dimension was clearly marked. For instance, the value of *care* was noted under several headings for the second half of the summer term: caring for ourselves (by being active, e.g. sports day); caring for others (who do we care for at home/school/other contexts? What does this involve? How does it make us feel to care for someone or something?); care linked to performance (taking care to perform at our best, being resilient so that I know that by pushing myself I get better at things).

Good planning is linked to careful formative assessment. At Beenham, pupils learn to assess their performance and progress as they journey through the curriculum. In the lesson about care, one boy said that he thought he should show care by playing with other boys, not just his close friends. To do this, he needed to challenge himself more and be more thoughtful. The teacher said that she would help him, which she hoped would assist him in developing his capacity to challenge himself. What all this shows is that values-based education is at the heart of all that the school is and does. It is the platform for learning, teaching and pupil assessment.

As I bring this chapter to an end, I hope that you can now appreciate that a values-based school requires a leader and leadership team who ensure that values are embedded in the curriculum. In such schools, all lessons will have a values focus as well as a learning intention. Pupils will be actively engaged in the curriculum and appreciate the process that is happening to them. This last point was given official recognition in a school by Ofsted, who, after inspecting Haydon Wick School (in Swindon), said: 'The school's emphasis on values is fully appreciated by pupils and they say it helps them make sensible choices in their lives.'

A poignant metaphor I use to describe a values-based school is to visualise a beautifully crafted fruit bowl into which we can place delicious fruits. The bowl represents the values-based philosophy and practices, whilst the fruits represent important aspects of the values curriculum, which may include Philosophy for Children, learning power and an enquiry-led curriculum, which foster personal awareness, intercultural understanding, social cohesion and social inclusion. I believe that this creates the kernel of a curriculum that is fit for purpose in the twenty-first century.

Some reflection points to ponder from this chapter:

- Whatever role you play in life (parent, teacher, business person), think about the values on which you base your own leadership. Reflect about the degree to which they are positive values (e.g. determination) or potentially limiting (e.g. caution).

- How do others see you as a leader? Is your own perception that of others? Having the confidence to discuss this will help you to be more self-aware.

- If you are a teacher, consider how you will embed values within the lessons for your class and influence the school's curriculum to be values-based.

- If you are a parent, consider how your child's school is embedding positive human values within it. The school's website should give you some clues or speak to a member of staff. A school governor or official may be able to help.

Chapter 15

Focus on community

I have always been as fascinated by curriculum and leadership, which we explored in the previous chapter, as I am with the next aspect of values-based education: community. I recommend that all aspiring values-based organisations focus their attention on community.

In Australia, I first came across the expression, 'the outward facing school'. What does this expression mean to you?

Pause ...

For me, it is an important term, because the outward facing school is one that sees itself as a part of an educational process that involves the wider community. A good example is illustrated in the experience of Salisbury High School (Adelaide). For adolescents to be committed to values-based education, the school realised that they needed to be fully engaged in *service learning*, a term used particularly in the United States and Australia. Service learning occurs when students become actively involved in community projects, sometimes involving school action teams, so that their learning is based on real-life situations. At Salisbury High School, the staff ensure that students are engaged in community projects and that their families are involved in the process too. Partnerships are set up in the community with local companies. For instance, the school set up a Year 10 robotics programme in partner-ship with an electronics company and the University of South Australia.

The impact of such values initiatives was thoroughly researched by Australia's University of Newcastle, which found that values education has a positive effect on schools and the community (Lovat et al., 2009). The study described how values education builds positive and wide-ranging connections between teachers, students and parents. Whilst it supported student engagement in learning, it also profoundly improved parent engagement in their children's learning, and allowed teachers to develop new relationships with their students, each other, parents and families in their school community. This was done through shared goals and practices in values education, which led to the development of mutual feelings of respect, trust and safety, and varied opportunities for collaboration. The research findings show that the focus on values led to improved, stronger relationships between teachers, students and parents. For instance, there were more respectful behaviours in the classroom, school and home. Community engagement led to quality outcomes for teachers, students and parents. The research highlighted the profound professional and personal transformation that can result when the parent community is involved in students' learning about values.

The establishment of communication about values between teachers, students, parents and the community – through newsletters, commu-nity forums and artistic performances – has very positive effects. For instance, giving time and space for teachers and parents to be involved in their children's values education both enhances relationships and affords time for parents to reflect on their own values. A values-based school is therefore an outward looking school. It works with and in the community. Parents, grandparents and other community members feel at ease in the school, and willingly contribute their talents and sup-port. The school, through an emphasis on schemes such as family values, encourages the whole family to explore values actively. The community and the media are informed about the school's values work, so that it spreads an understanding of its relevance and potency.

I was made aware of a great example of values being integral to family and community development at Sandylands School (in Morecambe). Katie Greenwood, the values coordinator, told me that values education is at the heart of everything they do at Sandylands. It is an integral part of the school's curriculum and they use the language of values as a tool to complement their teaching. They use values as a method of involving parents in their children's social and emotional learning; the parents are now more confident and actively seek out teachers to discuss how their child is using a value and how they can support them. Katie says:

> At Sandylands, we are most proud of the way our children have responded to becoming a values-based school. They understand the importance of positive values and know they are principles that they can use to guide them in their day-to-day lives. Our children are excellent ambassadors in the community for the work we do. They are enthusiastic about our values-based community projects and regularly suggest ideas on how to incorporate values-based work in our curriculum. Our work in values education has created a lasting legacy in our community. We regularly receive fantastic feedback from families and people within the community, such as local businesses, who say that, because the children of Sandylands are encouraged to live their values in the community, they have a very clear understanding of the impact of any decisions they make. We strongly believe this is due to the effectiveness of values education in developing knowledge, skills and attitudes that enable children to grow into stable, educated and civilised adults.

During a visit to Sandylands, Katie and Allison Hickson, the head teacher, demonstrated many examples of how the children's community awareness and involvement had increased because of the school's focus on living the school's values. Allison described how a group of children told the school's Parliament that they had noticed that the town's war memorial was falling into disrepair. They were upset that respect was not being shown to the memory of those who had died. The Parliament decided that the children should write to the town council to raise their concerns and to ask for money to be given for its repair. The council replied that unfortunately there had been financial cutbacks and they could not afford to repair the memorial.

The children were not discouraged and decided to raise money for its repair. They organised various fund-raising events, such as cake sales, to which they invited their parents and members of the community. The children raised a magnificent £1,500, which they presented to the council. Morecambe's war memorial is now repaired because of the children at Sandylands School. Allison passionately remarked:

> When I think of values education I think of the value of simplicity. It embodies the very thing that made us choose education as our pathway. In this world of competition, targets and political spin it provides us with a framework to develop active citizens who will seek fairness and equality for all.

> The response from our community has been amazing and more than we could ever have dreamed of. Sandylands is a place where you see smiling faces and a sense that everyone is in it together no matter how difficult the things are that we have to face. Values education is not an extra in the hidden curriculum but clear and focused. We have seen pupils' confidence grow and children at risk of failure flourishing. I find it a privilege to work for a community that is written off by many. I know that, with strong values, the next generation will bring a sense of humanity, which will give them the courage to work for what they believe in.

Not far away from Morecambe, at Revoe School (in Blackpool), I talked to a parent about the effects of being part of a family values scheme. The school invites parents to work with their children, sometimes at school, on values projects. On the day of my visit, a small group of mums were working experientially with their children on the value of respect. They were adding to their logbooks to show how they had been thinking about respect. I asked one of the mums what she liked about the family values scheme. She said: 'It gives us a chance to work together with our children. I would encourage all schools to do this because it teaches children to be more honest and respectful.' I asked what difference it had made to her family and she replied: 'A very big difference, very big. Basically my girls were playing up at home, no respect for mum. It has turned them round completely. Love it!'

In the south of England, the Elmbridge Partnership of schools in Surrey worked together on a mission to take values into the local community. The nine schools (two secondaries, one special and six primaries) have mounted exhibitions called 'Values for our Community'. These have included a family values arts project and a poetry project. The exhibitions have been mounted in the town centre with students and staff engaging with local residents about the importance of values in the community.

Wilds Lodge Therapeutic School (in Rutland) is a residential values school for boys between the ages of seven and eighteen, whose behaviour currently excludes them from mainstream schooling. The school brings the community to it: events such as an annual music festival give the boys the opportunity to invite mainstream schools to join with them and play at the festival, which the pupils and staff organise. I have found this school inspirational because the teaching and care staff demonstrate how a values-based approach really does affect behaviour at a practical level. The students go home at the weekends and, in one of the dormitories, I noticed a piece of card cut out in the shape of a suitcase. On it were written the values that a boy thought he should take home with him. He had written in big letters: *honest, kind, cooperate, fun, love, sensible* and *safe*.

The effect of a values approach on parents was brought home to me during a visit to Lyneham Primary School (in Wiltshire). A parent asked to see me to share her family's experience with values. She told me that it had made a big difference to the quality of their relationships. She explained that when the family went for a day out to a theme park or zoo, they took yellow cards with them, similar to warning cards shown to players at a soccer match. If the children were beginning to behave inappropriately they would be shown a yellow card, which reminded them to stop and think about their behaviour. I listened to the parent as she enthusiastically shared her process with me. I remember thinking that her scheme lacked something if it was really a balanced values approach. I was reassured completely, however, when she exclaimed, 'Of course, the children can, and do, hold up yellow cards to me and my husband!'

Parents are very much the focus for Sue Cahill, the values/well-being leader at St Charles Borromeo School (in Melbourne). Sue ensures that the school has strong, practical, daily links with parents and the community. Parents seek her out to share their natural worries and concerns about their child's development at school. Sue liaises with other members of staff and the principal. For instance, Sue describes how a grandfather came to see her to let her know that his daughter, the mother of two pupils at the school, had been hospitalised. Sue then mediated with the children's classroom teachers, informed the principal and met with the children to see that they were settled.

Another example is when a parent met with Sue to talk about new court orders regarding the shared care of their child due to the separation of the parents. Sue informed the classroom teacher and, because the child seemed anxious, informed the principal. Sue met with the child to make sure she was coping with the new living arrangements. Sue then contacted the parents individually to let them know how their child was managing. This partnership between school and family is a trusting one that benefits all, but particularly the child. I picked up a great idea from Sue: values fridge magnets. These are small, attractively designed, magnetic posters displaying the school's values, such as, 'We agree to live by our values of: confidence, responsibility, tolerance and courage …'

I have seen some great ideas to help families think about the importance of values. For instance, at Praslin airport (Seychelles), a picture of a child greets visitors on a large hoarding (sponsored by Cable & Wireless), which boldly states: 'Cultivating values in your child is the best investment you can make for his/her future.' In Surrey, Oatlands Infant School has huge values banners hanging outside the school building. Along with the school's magnificent values sculpture (see

Chapter 2), these make a powerful statement to the community about the importance of values. Another example is of a sculpture, which my wife, Jane, and I were honoured to unveil at Clehonger School (in Herefordshire). It was designed by a pupil, Jess Hedges, and created by local sculptor, Gwynne Williams, who worked his magic from Jess's design and produced a wonderful bronze statuette:

It depicts a parent holding up a child, who is holding up the world – a wonderful metaphor for the potential power of values. Sue Jones, the head teacher says: 'It represents values education and how it helps us to lift our children and give them the emo-tional strength to go on and support the world as positive citizens of a global community. Values education is the single most important aspect of our school.'

Specially designed values gardens can also engage the imagination of the community, examples of which can be seen at Clehonger School and Hinchley Wood Primary School (in Surrey). Both gardens were designed and built by parents and members of the local community as a creative expression of the schools' values.

In this chapter, my aim has been to share with you both the rationale and some practical examples that illustrate how values-based schools can inspire and enable the whole community to embrace values-based education. They reflect my belief that the school is a microcosm of the world – that what is created in school today can provide a glimpse of how our world can be tomorrow. I hope you feel inspired too.

Some reflection points to ponder from this chapter:

- Consider some ways that you could encourage your community to embrace values-based education. What practical steps can you take to bring this about?

- If you are involved in business or other activities, can you support your local school to embrace, in partnership with you, an aspect of values-based education?

- If you work in a school, is it an outward facing school? Can you encourage a greater community focus so that there is a deeper partnership between staff, parents and the community in general?

Chapter 16

Focus on values assessment

I have enjoyed supporting a growing group of values-based head teachers/principals and teachers worldwide. Simon Cowley, currently the head teacher of Haydon Wick School (in Swindon) readily springs to mind. This is because Simon's leadership of the school demonstrates a number of dispositions which I think are important in creating a school community that embraces excellent practices and appropriate management systems. These include: vision, deep listening, reflection, clear inclusive decision-making and a focus on assessment. The last of these, assessment, is fundamental and therefore the subject of this chapter, because it ensures that the teaching and learning practices (pedagogy) of values-based schools are judged to be aspects of *quality education.*

What does the term *assessment* currently mean to you? Please take a few moments to reflect on this question before continuing reading.

Pause ...

My understanding is that assessment includes regular monitoring of the curriculum and periodic evaluations of its effectiveness. I have seen assessments conducted by pupils, staff, school officials, school governors/boards and external inspection agencies, such as Ofsted (England) or Estyn (Wales). Whilst in the process of writing this book, Simon (see his photo below) sent me extracts from Ofsted's inspection of Haydon Wick. The school had been judged to be in the category of outstanding and had been recognised for its quality work in values-based education. The report included statements such as: 'The school's emphasis on values is fully appreciated by pupils and they say it helps them make sensible choices in their lives.'

I was not surprised to read such remarks, because a few months previously I had visited Haydon Wick to conduct an assessment of the school for the International Values Education Trust's Quality Mark. I had seen for myself how the school thoroughly planned and assessed its practices, and had established an engaging curriculum supported by excellent teaching. I was delighted to award the Quality Mark and talk at a meeting of parents about why the school had achieved this recognition.

Simon describes the values-based approach of the school:

> The quality of teaching is outstanding at Haydon Wick because the staff continuously reflect on their own values and how these impact on learning. At Haydon Wick, our values-based approach creates a positive atmosphere that touches each and every person. The importance of modelling our core values sets the tone for all that we do. Since the introduction of values-based education, pupils now have a heightened awareness of the needs of others and how values contribute to developing per-sonal contentment.

Haydon Wick represents one of a growing number of UK schools that are being recognised by external inspection services, such as Ofsted, for the excellence of their values work and the contribution this makes to quality education. Here are two further examples from Ofsted reports of schools in mixed catchment areas:

Washingborough Academy, Lincolnshire:

The behaviour and safety of pupils are outstanding. Pupils demonstrate excellent attitudes to work in lessons. They value adults' support and show respect for them. Pupils relate with each other very well. Behaviour is impeccable and is consistently well managed. This demonstrates the school's success with its planned programme for helping pupils to understand the importance of values (ideas that guide the choices they make and their behaviour) in their lives. Parents, staff and pupils rightly feel that this approach has created an exceptionally positive climate for learning.

Broughton Fields Primary School, Milton Keynes:

Pupils show extremely positive attitudes to learning across the school. This contributes well to the faster progress seen in school. The staff help pupils to take pride in the school, creating a calm, friendly and engaging classroom environment. There is a very clear behaviour policy and strong moral code that is based on 'values'. Pupils are respectful and value each other and show good manners towards all adults and each other. Themes such as cooperation and sharing are emphasised in assemblies and in lessons. Playground and classroom behaviour is impeccable.

In my view, assessment is an integral part of values-based education and needs to be built into the planning, implementation and review processes for quality assurance. When I worked as a head teacher, I used staff, pupil and parent surveys, including transcribed interviews, to give me a detailed understanding of the way that values-based education was being perceived as a positive cultural transformational tool and whether it was improving the quality of education in the school. To aid my analysis, I also used the information from lesson observations by myself and other staff to inform our understanding of the effects of values education, both on the school and its community. Ofsted, local authority inspectors and other invited assessors provided external school evaluation, which complemented our internal evaluation and informed the planning process. I also felt that research could be a great aid and stimulus for school development, so I welcomed various researchers (including me!) to look at the school's work and life, so that we could use the evidence to improve our curriculum.

Many schools are finding, as I did, that hearing the pupil voice is an important part of assessment. I recall having the pleasure of interviewing Sam Gardner in 1999, when he was eleven, about what he thought he was learning from West Kidlington School's emphasis on values. By this time, he had experienced six years of values education. Sam said:

> If I did not know about values, I would not be such a nice person to know. I think that children put a lot of effort into learning about values and being nice. I am not saying that people who do not know about values cannot be nice, because they can. It helps to make life easier if you know about values and it comes more naturally to be nice. At this school, I feel I am a part of a big community where everybody is loving and caring.

Recently, I interviewed Sam again during a values conference in Oxford, at which he had agreed to speak. I asked him what he now remembered about values education – his answer brought tears of joy to my eyes:

> I remember the people, the staff ... there was something different about them, different about their relationships with us that made us feel equal. They weren't over-familiar or wanted to be like our friends ... they just modelled the school's values – they were an inspiration. We wanted to be like these people. They were totally committed to the values, not just teaching them, they were living them.

For me, such remarks are the most poignant assessment of values-based education as they show its powerful, lasting effects. Asking children to reflect about their ongoing experience helps them to think about its effects, and reinforces the positive messages about how to relate to yourself and others, and focus attention on learning.

Here are some quotes from pupils talking about values at Oatlands Infant School (in Surrey). It is interesting to see the progression of understanding; how much more embedded the values are with the older Year 2 children. They have absorbed the language and the values, and are more able to talk about them in terms of themselves. The younger Year 1 children are still reflecting the adults' language and mostly talk about values in terms of other people. This certainly indicates the importance of returning to the values on a two-year cycle, as well as always keeping them high profile.

Year 1 pupils

Trev: Values help people learn that there are rules that you have to follow, otherwise some things can go wrong. I like respect because then people know that you shouldn't push or hit and you need to be kind. Values help us all to be safe and happy.

Louisa: Values help me to be nice to my family.

Jessica: I use values in the playground, in class and at home. My favourite values are love and respect. I respect my little brothers. Values help me to be happy.

Year 2 pupils

Emily: Values help me to think carefully when I am going to do something wrong. I think of the values and say I shouldn't do that. Values help me to learn. Values help me to be happy. When someone is not being nice, I use values to stand up for myself – I am nice to them and they just stop.

Amy: Values help me to understand things I find difficult. If I am doing learning and I can't get it right, I think of a value and I get it right, because they help me calm down and not get angry. Values help me to be responsible for things and they give me the courage to try new things.

Theo: Values help me to play gently – I think of love and then I play more gently if I know I am getting rough. I use understanding a lot. I understand when other people are feeling hurt.

Jessica: Values are important to me because if we didn't have them we wouldn't be as happy or gentle or respectful as we are – we all have a much better time because we do the values. I think happiness is the best value. If every school had values, our lives would be happier. Values help you to remember to be thoughtful and nice.

These children's comments fill my heart with joy and a sense of hope for the future; a hope that is being fuelled by the outstanding work of schools and colleges around the world. Wellington College (in Berkshire), an independent, co-educational day and boarding secondary school, has created an innovative curriculum that puts equal emphasis on personal, social and academic development – emphasising the well-being and happiness of each student. The master is Dr Anthony Seldon, who is well known as an outstanding educational and political commentator. He is celebrated for his biographies of British Prime Ministers Tony Blair and John Major. Often quoted in the media for his respected views on educational issues, Anthony Seldon enthusiastically endorses values-based education:

At Wellington College, we believe that education is only of enduring meaning if it is underpinned by profound values: the five which our community itself has chosen being courage, integrity, respect, kindness and responsibility. I believe that values-based education should be the driving principle for all schools and colleges in the twenty-first century.

You will gather that my vision is for values-based education to become the driving principle for all schools, organisations, communities and countries in the twenty-first century. I hope that reading this book is inspiring you to become an active part of this movement for positive change.

Please pause now and mull over what insights you have gained from reading this chapter.

Pause ...

My aim has been to underline the importance of the assessment of values-based education. Without the benefits of assessment, it would be too easy for detractors to dismiss it as just about the development of the so-called 'soft skills' of character development, and lacking in academic rigour and proven benefits. Therefore, whatever organisation you work in, I think it is very important to regularly assess and reflect on what is happening.

From my own experience, I have found that if there is an absence of quality assessment then a gap can grow between what is perceived to be happening and what is actually happening. To guard against this, the assessment-focused school monitors (and celebrates) values-based education and evaluates its effectiveness. It is able to articulate and demonstrate why values based education is synonymous with quality education. To aid this process, carefully constructed surveys are given to pupils and parents to measure its efficacy. Values education is reported to parents in pupil reports and governors/school boards receive regular reports on the school's values dimension. The school gathers and monitors data for evidence of its effectiveness, ensuring continuous improvement in values education. It is open to scrutiny and research. It considers having a goal, such as working towards the International Values Education Trust's Quality Mark, which gives added focus for improving provision.

To achieve such high standards, I recommend that all adults in school be provided with informed, sustained and targeted professional learning, and appropriately fostered professional collaborations.

Some reflection points to ponder from this chapter:

- Having read this chapter, what does assessment of values-based education now mean to you?

- How do you intend to monitor and evaluate values-based education in your setting?

- What will you do to share your achievements and celebrate your successes?

Chapter 17

From my heart

We have reached the final chapter of our journey together. I have shared with you the philosophy and a range of key practices of values-based education, which I hope have inspired you. Do you recall how our journey began? I invited you to have a virtual relationship with me. This is because I believe that we best learn about values in supportive relationships; hence, I focus on the importance of the values-based family, school, business and community. It is through meaningful relationships that our values are nurtured. This relational process can then fuel our sense of meaning and purpose, helping us to develop a secure sense of self – a precursor for living a happy and fulfilling life. As you have discovered from the examples I have given, living by positive values can give us a moral compass to navigate successfully the ups and downs of our increasingly complex lives.

I want now to speak to you from my heart. For many years, I have been acutely aware that my life's purpose is intrinsically rooted in the understanding that, if humankind is to flourish, then there is a need for each of us to live life on the basis of embracing universal, positive human values, such as honesty, compassion, respect, tolerance, trust, justice and peace. From this appreciation, I have concluded that a peaceful, harmonious world can only emerge if the core values of love, justice and peace live in each one of us and are expressed in our behaviour. Is this possible? When times are easy, it is not so difficult to love, but when, for instance, our survival is challenged, afflictive emotions, such as fear, influence our psyche and we can behave inappropriately, either individually or collectively, or in violent ways (verbally and physically) towards others. At such difficult times – we all have them – we need the ability to turn off the automatic pilot of our habitual thinking and responses, and instead to be guided by the compass of our values.

As people and events have influenced your life, so have the people, relationships, circumstances and events of my life's journey greatly influenced and helped to form my character. Four personal stories – one inspirational, two that challenged my view of humanity and one that touched my heart – stand out in my mind. I think that if I share them with you, then you will have a clearer understanding about what has influenced the development of my own values. In turn, I invite you to reflect on what has formed your own.

The first event happened when I was a very small boy, lying in bed, conscious of hearing the news on television in the adjacent room. I could hear gunfire and shouting, which disturbed me, so I crept out of bed and nervously peeped through the gap in living room door, unnoticed by my family. I felt anxious as I saw soldiers and tanks in the streets of a city. People were throwing bottles that exploded on the tanks. There were distressing scenes of bodies piled in disrespectful heaps along a roadside. The scenes were deeply upsetting and I had no understanding about what was going on, except that it must be real because it was a part of the evening news. I crept back to bed and remember worrying that the tanks would soon be outside our home and that we would all be killed. I talked to my grandmother, who lived with us, the next day about my fears. She said that it was very sad because the Russians had just invaded Hungary and many people had been killed. I was left with a feeling of total confusion and sadness.

The year was 1956, the year of the Hungarian Uprising and subsequent crushing. These events were not discussed openly in Hungary until the end of the Cold War, thirty years later. They have continued to live with me and often surface in my consciousness to remind me of the evil of violence, and to be aware of any tendencies that I may have to act from a place of anger, blame or intolerance. Also, it reminds me of the impact that ruptured relationships, either in the home or in the community, have on a child's sense of well-being.

My second personal story has had a profound impact on my thinking. It occurred at the time when I was invited to be interviewed for my first school headship. I had been encouraged by Jack Crump, the local education officer, to apply for the headship of a small village school at Oakley Green, which is situated just outside the town of Windsor. The interviews were to take place at 2 p.m. in the education offices in Windsor with the school's governors. Being somewhat nervous, I arrived in the town in the morning and decided to pass the time visiting Windsor's famous castle. I soon became swept along with a flood of excited tourists representing many countries.

Needing a quiet reflective space, I wandered into St George's Chapel, and enjoyed its still and peaceful atmosphere. After a few minutes, I found myself viewing the memorial to George VI (who was the subject of the 2010 film *The King's Speech*). My eyes were drawn to a brass plaque on which was written part of a poem by Minnie Louise Haskins known as 'The Gate of the Year'. Apparently, it first caught the public attention and popular imagination after the king's daughter, Princess Elizabeth (the current queen), handed a copy to her father, which he quoted in his 1939 Christmas broadcast to the British Empire.

The poem was widely acclaimed as inspirational. Its words had an instant and lasting impact on me, not because of any religious connotation, but because they gave me the permission, inspiration and courage to speak my truth with confidence at the interview. I recall describing what I thought were the ingredients of a successful school. I was appointed. If you ever visit the chapel at Windsor Castle you will see that the words on the brass plaque read:

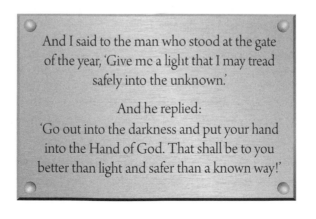

And I said to the man who stood at the gate of the year, 'Give me a light that I may tread safely into the unknown.'

And he replied:
'Go out into the darkness and put your hand into the Hand of God. That shall be to you better than light and safer than a known way!'

The powerful advice was an *aha!* moment for me, a moment of realisation, which reminded me to be my authentic self; that I must continue to trust in the truth of my developing philosophy, and not be distracted by those who don't appreciate its relevance and power as a force for good in the world. Today, it continues to remind me to guard against acting from my ego (self-interest), which sometimes has a tendency to want to be noticed – not being interested in altruism. Instead, I set my sights on working towards fulfilling my meaning and purpose.

The third story from my own life is set during a visit to Israel with a group of teachers. As part of our visit, we were taken to Yad Vashem, the Jewish memorial to the Holocaust. I recall opening a door and walking into an underground cavern, which at first appeared to be pitch black. It was the Children's Memorial, a unique tribute to approximately 1.5 million Jewish children who perished during the Holocaust. Memorial candles, a customary Jewish tradition to remember the dead, are reflected infinitely in a dark and sombre space, creating the impression of millions of stars shining in the firmament.

The names of murdered children, their ages and countries of origin can be heard being recited in the background. As I re-emerged into the sunlight, the simple power of this heart-rending experience fired a determination in me to focus my energy on supporting children to develop as humane people, which I think is even, dare I say it, more important than the subjects of schooling. My thoughts reminded me of the words of Haim Ginott in his book, *Teacher and Child* (1976). He shares a letter, provided to all the teachers in a school on the first day of class by their principal. It reads as follows:

Dear Teacher,

I am the survivor of a concentration camp. My eyes saw what no person should witness: Gas chambers built by learned engineers. Children poisoned by educated physicians. Infants killed by trained nurses. Women and babies shot and burned by high school and college graduates. So I am suspicious of education.

My request is: Help your students become human. Your efforts must never produce learned monsters, skilled psychopaths, educated Eichmanns. Reading, writing and arithmetic are important only if they serve to make our children more humane.

Your Principal

I am convinced that values-based education makes a huge contribution to helping students to be more humane, as it does in helping them to develop intellectual curiosity, communicative competence, academic diligence and other aspects which we would describe as the outcome of being educated.

My final story underlines the joy of being a teacher and the influence that the vocation can have on the lives of others. It relives an incident when I was a class teacher at Wroughton Junior School (in Swindon) in the early stages of my career. I remember a petite, eight-year-old girl in my class called Sarah.

The head teacher had informed me that she was an elective mute, so I was not to worry if she remained silent, but perhaps I could influence her to talk. Sarah came to school every day and maintained her silence. No one seemed to know why she had decided to be mute. Her mother said that she used to speak, but after a family dispute she had stopped communicating. It was suspected by a school psychologist that Sarah had found a method of control. Days and weeks went by and I seemed to be building a good relationship with Sarah; she sometimes smiled at my humour but she remained silent. The children in the class were supportive and seemed to accept Sarah's silence. I remember that we were engaged in a creative, enquiry-based project on our local community. The pupils were enthused to find out more about their locality by interviewing their parents, grandparents and neighbours. I lent the pupils voice-recording machines and one had gone home with Sarah. Lots of artefacts were brought to school, heirlooms from a past age, which made a fascinating historical display.

One morning, Sarah came into class early, knowing that I would be there, and smiling. She stretched out her hands in which she was holding her voice-recording machine. She thrust it into my hands and hurriedly left the room. I quizzically switched the machine on and I heard a quiet voice saying, 'Hello Mr. Hawkes, I am speaking to you from behind our settee at home. You see, I can speak! Thank you for being kind and nice to me. I promise I will try to speak at school.' When she came back into the classroom, I quietly thanked her and gave her a knowing smile. When I had heard Sarah's voice, it brought tears of joy to my eyes as I realised what a great job teaching is; that by building a secure uncritical relationship, I had helped Sarah to find an inner strength to rejoin the speaking world.

On parents' consultation evening, her parents acknowledged that the school had been the catalyst for Sarah speaking again. They told me that she now almost didn't stop talking! For me as a young teacher, the message I took from this event was that good relationships are the foundation for positively influencing and inspiring young people to be the best people they can possibly become – the foundation of values-based education.

I hope you can now appreciate, through the telling of these four stories, why my life's purpose is to influence the adoption of values-based education in all aspects of society. I hope too that the stories resonate with aspects of your own experience. May I encourage you to tell your tales to others, because it is through story that we learn the important things about what it means to be human and share what is really important to us.

One of the reasons I promote values-based education is that I am aware that an increasing number of children, because of the breakdown of extended families, are coming to school without the richness that comes from hearing the stories of who we are, how we should live with each other and the values that should underpin our lives. The values-based school provides this knowledge, and other values-driven organisations can support and make huge contributions to the philosophy and practice in other areas of society.

Linda Heppenstall, an inspirational former teacher at West Kidlington School, was interviewed as part of a video produced by the school about values-based education. I often recall what she said, which accurately reflects my own understanding of this philosophy:

> What we really wanted for our school was to have a calm and purposeful environment where the children could develop their relationships; so that they could become reflective learners. We feel that all the work that we are doing with all the values in school helps them to do that ... When we first started this, we looked at what we felt the children needed and what we discovered was, what the children needed, the adults here did too! They needed to feel valued as individuals; they needed to feel supported when they had difficulties; they needed to feel loved; they needed to feel that they could express themselves creatively and grow academically too ... I am sure the children don't see us as some authority figure in the distance; they feel that they can talk to us, and we will treat them with respect and equality ...
>
> For the future, I really would hope we can develop the children as people, rather than think of them coming to school to be given aspects of the curriculum; be given more maths; be given more literacy; be given more science lessons. Yes, they are important, but I think that other things are more important first.

What of my vision for the future? On a visit to Hong Kong in 2008, I shared with my friend, Chris Drake, a lawyer and a keen supporter of values-based education, that I was founding a charity and asked him if he would be a trustee. I revealed to him my thoughts about the International Values Education Trust, which would be totally independent of any political or religious affiliation. It would promote a new understanding and framework to help people achieve constructive and purposeful lives for themselves and their communities, by engaging with positive values to guide and inform their behaviour. This approach would offer an innovative way of thinking about education in the home, school and community. It would also challenge and inform how business, commerce and politics should be conducted.

The task of the charity would be to spread the benefits of values-based education, and thereby help people to become successful and happy members of our global society. Chris enthusiastically agreed to be a trustee and others quickly followed. IVET now has an eclectic group of trustees, patrons and associates, who are working to the common goal of encouraging individuals, institutions and communities to be values-based. It is rapidly becoming known as a movement for positive change, and is forging partnerships with other like-minded charities and organisations, such as the Barrett Values Centre.

I hope that you have enjoyed hearing aspects of my story and learning from the practices of so many remarkable people who have embraced values-based education. My hope now is that you will want to be involved in supporting values-based education in whatever setting you find yourself. You can find out more at: www.valuesbasededucation. com.

The picture of me on the cover of this book is from a photo taken by Paddy Boyle when I addressed the National Association of Principals and Deputy Principals (NAPD) at Killarney (in Ireland). Clive Byrne, the energetic and charismatic director of NAPD, had invited me to Ireland following my address to the European School Heads Association in Cyprus. NAPD provided a memorable occasion where I experienced the special warmth, enthusiasm, humour and spiritual energy of the members of this Irish secondary school principals association.

I was later gladdened to read how my message had been embraced by Derek West in an article entitled, 'A Unique and Intimate Exchange of Thought and Feeling', which appeared in the association's journal, *Le Chéile*. Derek had caught and expressed the essence of values-based education. It is this essence, with its clarion call that is both simple yet profound – *respond to life from the self that embraces positive values* – that is firing the imagination of so many teachers, parents and community members worldwide.

The human spirit is yearning to be released from the shackles of our automatic pilot, with its habitual, ego-centred behavioural responses that can dominate us all, and which so often lead to stress and unhappiness. *Carpe diem*; we need to seize this moment. I believe that we are at an exciting point in human development, one that invites each one of us to embrace an altruistic, spiritual and intellectual leap of consciousness that will ensure we all continue to flourish. I am convinced that values-based education gives us a means that will help us to achieve this goal. At the conference in Ireland, I concluded my talk with the words of William Butler Yeats, from his poem 'He Wishes for the Cloths of Heaven'. I would like to share them with you:

> Had I the heavens' embroidered cloths,
> Enwrought with golden and silver light,
> The blue and the dim and the dark cloths
> Of night and light and the half-light,
> I would spread the cloths under your feet:
> But I, being poor, have only my dreams;
> I have spread my dreams under your feet;
> Tread softly because you tread on my dreams.

I have spread my dreams under your feet, and I am quietly confident that you will seek to embrace them in your personal and professional lives. Now over to you …

Some reflection points to ponder from this concluding chapter:

1   How do you use the events of your life that have specially impacted on you in a positive way?

2   In what ways has this book inspired you?

3   What actions will you now take in your personal and professional life to support values-based education?

Bibliography

Barrett, Richard (2010). *The New Leadership Paradigm: Leading Self, Leading Others, Leading and Organization, Leading in Society.* Fulfilling Books.

Barrett, Richard (2012). *Love, Fear and the Destiny of Nations.* Fulfilling Books.

Brown, David, Hamston, Julie, Weston, Jane and **Wajsenberg, Jenny** (2010). *Giving Voice to the Impacts of Values Education: The Final Report of the Values in Action Schools Project.* Carlton South: Education Services Australia.

Buber, Martin M. (1970). *I and Thou,* tr. Walter Kaufman. New York: Charles Scribner's Sons.

Buber, Martin M. (1973). *Meetings,* tr. Maurice Friedman. La Salle, IL: Open Court Publishing.

Commonwealth of Australia (2005). *National Framework for Values Education in Australian Schools.* Canberra: Department of Education and Training.

Dalai Lama (1999). *Ancient Wisdom, Modern World.* London: Little, Brown and Company.

Delors, Jacques et al. (1996). *Learning: The Treasure Within.* Report to UNESCO of the International Commission on Education for the Twenty-First Century. Paris: UNESCO.

Duckworth, Julie (2009). *The Little Book of Values.* Carmarthen: Crown House Publishing.

Farrer, Frances (2000). *A Quiet Revolution: Encouraging Positive Values in Our Children.* London: Random.

Fuller, Andrew (2007). *Tricky Kids: Transforming Conflict and Freeing Their Potential.* Sydney: Finch.

Fuller, Andrew (2011). *Life: A Guide.* Sydney: Finch.

Frankl, Viktor E. (1959). *Man's Search for Meaning.* Boston, MA: Beacon Press.

Ginott, Haim G. (1976). *Teacher and Child: A Book for Parents and Teachers.* New York: Macmillan.

Halstead, J. Mark and **Taylor, Monica J.** (2000). *The Development of Values, Attitudes and Personal Qualities: A Review of Recent Research.* Slough: National Foundation for Educational Research.

Hanh, Thich Nhat (1975). *The Miracle of Mindfulness,* tr. Mobi Ho. Boston, MA: Beacon Press.

Hawkes, Neil (2003). *How to Inspire and Develop Values in your Classroom.* Cambridge: LDA.

Hawkes, Neil (2010). *Does Teaching Values Improve the Quality of Education in Primary Schools? A Study about the Impact of Introducing Values Education in a Primary School.* Beau-Bassin, Mauritius: VDM Publishing House.

Hay, Julie (1995). *Donkey Bridges for Developmental TA: Making Transactional Analysis Memorable and Accessible.* Watford: Sherwood Publishing.

Hobson, Peter R. (2001). 'Aristotle, 384–382 BCE'. In Joy A. Palmer, Liora Bresler and David Cooper (eds), *Fifty Major Thinkers on Education: From Confucius to Dewey.* London: Routledge, pp. 14–19.

Layard, Richard and **Dunn, Judy** (2009). *A Good Childhood: Searching for Values in a Competitive Age. A Landmark Report for the Children's Society.* London: Penguin.

Lovat, Terence J., Toomey, Ron, Dally, Kerry and **Clement, Neville** (2009). *Project to Test and Measure the Impact of Values Education on Student Effects and School Ambience.* Report for the Australian Government Department of Education, Employment and Workplace Relations by the University of Newcastle Australia. Canberra: DEEWR.

Lovat, Terence J., Toomey, Ron and **Clement, Neville** (eds) (2010). *International Research Handbook on Values Education and Student Wellbeing.* Berlin: Springer.

McGettrick, Bart (1995). *Values and Educating the Whole Person.* Edinburgh: Scottish Consultative Council on the Curriculum.

McLaughlin, Terence H. and **Halstead J. Mark** (1999). 'Education in Character and Virtue'. In J. Mark Halstead and Terence H. McLaughlin (eds), *Education in Morality.* London: Routledge, pp. 136–162.

Martin, Jane R. (2001). 'Maria Montessori, 1870–1952'. In Joy A. Palmer, Liora Bresler and David Cooper (eds), *Fifty Major Thinkers on Education: From Confucius to Dewey.* London: Routledge, pp. 224–228.

Montessori, Maria (1972). *The Montessori Method.* Chicago, IL: Henry Regnery.

Morgan, Nicola S., Ellis, Gill and Reid, Ken (2012). *Better Behaviour through Home-School Relations: Using Values-Based Education to Promote Positive Learning.* London: Routledge.

Morris, Ian (2009). *Teaching Happiness and Well-Being in Schools: Learning to Ride Elephants.* London: Continuum.

Noddings, Nel (1992). *The Challenge to Care in Schools.* New York: Teachers College Press.

Rodger, Alex (1996). *Developing Moral Community in a Pluralist School Setting.* Aberdeen: Gordon Cook Foundation.

Scharmer, C. Otto (2009). *Theory U: Leading from the Future as it Emerges.* San Francisco, CA: Berrett-Koehler.

Siegel, Daniel J. (2007). *The Mindful Brain: Reflection and Attunement in the Cultivation of Well-Being.* New York: W. W. Norton & Co.

Senge, Peter M., Scharmer, C. Otto, Jaworski, Joseph and **Flowers, Betty Sue** (2004). *Presence: Human Purpose and the Field of the Future.* Boston, MA: Nicholas Brealey.

Tillman, Diane (2001). *Living Values Activities for Children Ages 8–14.* Deerfield, FL: Health Communications Inc.

Tillman, Diane (2001). *Living Values Activities for Young Adults.* Deerfield, FL: Health Communications, Inc.

Tillman, Diane (2001). *Living Values Parents Groups: A Facilitator Guide.* Deerfield, FL: Health Communications, Inc.

Tillman, Diane and **Hsu, Diana** (2001). *Living Values Activities for Children Ages 3–7.* Deerfield, FL: Health Communications, Inc.

Tillman, Diane and **Quera Colomina, Pilar** (2001). *LVEP Educator Training Guide.* Deerfield, FL: Health Communications, Inc.

Waters, Mick (2013). *Thinking Allowed: On Schooling.* Carmarthen: Independent Thinking Press.

West, Derek (2012). 'A Unique and Intimate Exchange of Thought and Feeling'. *Le Chéile: Journal of the National Association of Principals and Deputy Principals,* No. 6, 48–61.

Wilkinson, Richard G. and **Pickett, Kate E.** (2009). *The Spirit Level.* London: Allen Lane.

Woodrow, Floyd and **Acland, Simon** (2012). *Elite! The Secret to Exceptional Leadership and Performance.* London: Elliott and Thompson.

Zimbardo, Philip G. and **Duncan, Nikita** (2012). *The Demise of Guys: Why Boys Are Struggling and What We Can Do About It.* New York: TED Conferences LLC.